CAREER PROFILES AND SEX DISCRIMINATION
in the Library Profession

Prepared
by
Kathleen M. Heim and Leigh S. Estabrook
for the
Committee on the Status of Women in Librarianship
American Library Association

Chicago 1983

AMERICAN LIBRARY ASSOCIATION

Library of Congress Cataloging in Publication Data

Heim, Kathleen M.
    Career profiles and sex discrimination in the
library profession.

    Bibliography: p.
    Includes index.
    1. Women librarians--United States. 2. Librarians--
Salaries, pensions, etc.--United States. 3. Librarians--
United States--Job descriptions. 4. Sex discrimination in
employment--United States. 5. Library surveys--United
States. I. Estabrook, Leigh S. II. Title.
Z682.H459   020'.88042   83-3838
ISBN 0-8389-3282-7

832238

Contents

Tables

Preface

On February 25, 1979, the Committee on the Status of Women
in Librarianship (COSWL) of the American Library Association
submitted a proposal for the J. Morris Jones and Bailey K.
Howard-World Book Encyclopedia-ALA Goal Awards for funding of
a pilot research project entitled "A Pilot Profile of the
Women Members of the American Library Association." The project received $5,000 from the Bailey K. Howard-World Book
Encyclopedia-ALA Goal Award. We were selected as principal
investigators.

The overall purpose of the COSWL study was to provide data
for evaluating the status of women in librarianship. Individual studies had shown a disproportionate number of men in
administrative positions in libraries and a significant difference between male and female librarians' salaries. There had
also been studies on individual factors such as mobility as a
means of explaining these salary and status inequities. No
study existed at that time which studied the relationship of
sex to status and salary, and a range of personal, demographic, and career patterns. The COSWL study sought to fill
this gap in research.

A complementary objective of the investigators was to design
a study that would contribute to the positive image of women
in librarianship by virtue of the quality of the research.
Attention to methodology was seen to be important to assure
that the study's findings would be taken seriously since criticism of methodology is one of the easiest ways to dismiss
research findings that are unpalatable. Moreover, if the research conducted by two women for the Committee on the Status
of Women in Librarianship was seen to be of high quality, it
was thought that some indirect benefits would accrue to that
Committee.

   Throughout the study we were fortunate to have the counsel, encouragement, and support of Margaret Myers from the Office for Library Personnel Resources of the American Library Association. The University of Illinois Graduate School of Library and Information Science provided telephone service, graduate student assistance, photocopying and secretarial service, acquisition of materials through interlibrary loan, and support for keypunching part of the data. Syracuse University School of Information Studies provided telephone service, computer time for data analysis, graduate student assistance, secretarial service, and monetary support to pay for coding and keypunching part of the data. The investigators were also fortunate to have the enthusiastic support of students and colleagues, several of whom worked extensively on the project without pay, academic credit, or any other reward than a deeply felt thank-you. Finally, we are grateful to the almost 2,000 librarians who took the time to answer the seven-page questionnaire. We hope they will agree that the significance of the results made the investment of their time worthwhile.

   The following report is divided into four sections: first, a review of relevant literature pertaining to librarianship; second, a discussion of the methodology of the COSWL study; third, an analysis of major findings of the study; and fourth, an examination of the policy implications of the findings, as well as suggestions for future research in the area of the status of women in librarianship. Appendixes include the bibliography and questionnaire.

   This final report is presented in a formal and technical fashion. The investigators see it as a document which may be used by individuals who wish to conduct their own research on topics related to this area or who wish to evaluate the analysis of the COSWL data. Readers who wish a more general account of the findings may consult the December 1980 issue of <u>American Libraries</u> and the summer 1981 <u>Drexel Library Quarterly</u> for articles by Estabrook and Heim. At this time it is anticipated that the data set will be placed in a data archive for public use. A codebook is available for use by researchers.[1]

Kathleen M. Heim
   Graduate School of Library and
   Information Science, University
   of Illinois, Urbana-Champaign
Leigh S. Estabrook
   School of Information Studies,
   Syracuse University

# Review of the Literature

The rationale for the COSWL study lay in the fact that no comprehensive career study of libraians had taken place. While many studies had examined some demographic data on librarians' careers in one type of library (public, special) or at one position level (directors, reference staff) or had looked at several key variables (mobility, personality), no comprehensive United States study had ever been conducted. A study that dealt with a number of these questions had been conducted in Canada (Fischer et al., n.d.) but not disseminated in any formal manner, with the exception of a short article on salary differential which appeared in <u>Emergency Librarian</u> (Cheda et al., 1978). Obtaining the more comprehensive report submitted to the Canada Council proved fascinating, for this ambitious study, which attempted an investigation of discrimination and motivational differences of a stratified cluster random sample of 851 Canadian librarians, was not available or even identifiable by the Canadian Library Association.[1]

A copy of the report was eventually obtained by writing directly to the authors. The study focused on current job status and rate of advancement; continuity of work career; job changes and promotions; overt role actions; covert role actions; role descriptions; perceived role compatibility and conflict. The <u>Emergency Librarian</u> summary of salary differential (Cheda et al., 1978), based on the fuller reports, discussed a number of important findings which helped to validate the development of the questionnaire and also provided a base for comparison of some variables. This summary, based on a sample of 667 librarians, found that two-thirds of these Canadian

librarians were female and were paid in the lower salary
ranges (63.5% earned under $14,999 compared to 46.2% of
the men), while men were paid in the higher ranges (24.6% of
the men earned more than $19,000 compared to only 9.3% of the
women).

The Canadian study tested traditional reasons offered to explain such differences (lower educational qualifications, low-
er-level positions, interrupted careers) as well as reasons
offered by employers for why women will accept lower pay (less
motivation, lower aspirations, and little career planning).
In spite of similar educations, men earned higher salaries
than women. Since one out of five men was a director, compared to one out of eight women, the "ghettoization" theory
explained some salary differential; that is, the clustering in
low-paying positions dragged down the overall median earning
for women. Answers to questions on interrupted careers revealed that motherhood and marriage did not deflect women librarians' careers and that career interruptions could not
explain salary differences. Motivation and aspiration were
measured by posing "six problems in the lives of others," and
asking respondents to choose answers. The questions were
evaluated in terms of upward mobility, and similar patterns
for male and female respondents were found.

Career planning was measured by assessing job seeking ef-
forts and willingness to move. Again, there was little difference in the response. The researchers concluded that none
of the controlling variables for sex explained the salary differential. The study ended with the comment, "It is true that
this does not prove discrimination, is at least a partial explanation, but it does eliminate so many of the most often offered explanations, that discrimination cannot be dismissed
lightly" (Fischer et al., n.d. p. 13).[2]

Margaret Slater's monograph Career Patterns and the Occupational Image (1979) reported on a study of British librarians
in 1977 and found that 71% of the library sample were female
and 29% male and 68% of the information sample were male and
32% female (a total of 312 were surveyed). A number of comparative tables present marital status, professional qualifications, position held, job tenure, and work experience.
Findings exploded the myth that maternity interferes with
women's careers. In fact maternity was less likely to take
women from the field than Armed Forces was to take men. This
study has interesting features for other variables examined
for the present study and will be discussed below.

Once Slater (British) and Fischer et al.(Canadian) were examined, there was no other comprehensive national level study
of libraries with which to work. The next step was to identify the various library studies which had been done in order
to obtain as clear a demographic picture of the field as possible at the outset.

THE LIBRARY UNIVERSE

Although no comprehensive analysis of U.S. librarians' careers exists, a number of studies provided demographic data which were of considerable importance as the COSWL survey instruments were developed. These underscored the central problem of female librarians: the dual structure of professional rewards for men and women. While in study after study women were found to dominate the work force in numbers and overall percentage, men earned higher salaries and held most administrative positions. In addition to this salient fact, the library profession tends to segregate by gender and type of work task, in that women gravitate to service roles or age-typed positions, such as school libraries and to children's work, while a disproportionately large number of men work in academic libraries and at administrative positions.

The COSWL study focused on ALA members, but the investigators felt it was important to understand the broadest definitions of library work for the career analysis portion of this study. The University of Pittsburgh Occupational Survey of Information Professionals (OSIP) (1980) estimated that 1.64 million individuals were involved in the information professions. Although the library work field accounted for only ten percent of the total, the OSIP study was important for its insights into the fringe area of library work. Indeed, the COSWL study did find that a growing percentage of ALA members are working outside of libraries.

Census data on librarians were analyzed in the report Library Manpower: A Study of Supply and Demand (U.S. Department of Labor, 1975), which is the most frequent source of demographic information used in analyses of the seventies library work force. This is the source often cited for the statement that the library profession is 84% female as well as the fact that nearly half of all individuals citing "librarian" as their occupation are employed in school settings. The 1980 census had not been conducted at the time of the survey for the present study, but more detailed research will be conducted by King Research for release in 1983. The methodology of the King Research study of library supply and demand as well as a summary of sources for employment information appear in the conceptual paper which will undergird this update to the 1975 report (DeWath and Cooper, 1980). These two reports are important information sources for the overall study of the library universe.

NEW GRADUATES

Examination of information on new library school graduates provided a better understanding of the pace of entry to the

library profession and a means of analyzing that subset of
individuals in the COSWL sample against the larger sample of
those entering the profession each year. The most comprehensive information on new graduates is collected by the American
Library Association for all levels of library training--Asso-
ciate of Arts to Ph.D. (American Library Association, Office
for Library Personnel Resources, n.d. and 1980). Data
collected by ALA/OLPR makes possible a comparison of male/fe-
male entrants as well as a study of minority group members
entering the field. The COSWL analyses used these data to determine if ALA was attracting new members in proportion to the
number entering the work force.

The _Library Journal_ series provides salary, sex, and type of
placement on a yearly basis for graduates of ALA-accredited
programs (Frarey and Learmont, 1973, 1974, 1975; Learmont and
Darling, 1976, 1977; Learmont and Troiano, 1979; Learmont,
1980). Because these data provide annual information on type
of placement, they are extremely valuable in analyzing changing work patterns.

Additional information on potential library personnel is
available on graduates of media programs, some of whom enter
the library field. While this information is not as complete
as that which appears in the _Library Journal_ series, it does
give some indication of the movement of media personnel into
new positions (Peterson, 1973, 1974, 1975, 1976, 1977; Sink,
1978, 1979, 1980). Next to the census data, the new graduate
information is the broadest available on the library work
force. It encompasses, or tries to encompass, the total new
graduate universe.

ASSOCIATION STUDIES

Association studies are made simple by the fact that membership lists are often computerized and universal or statistical
sampling may be conducted with relative ease. Since the COSWL
study is an example of such an effort, it was important to examine these studies to validate questions and to ensure as
much compatibility as possible among studies. There has been,
to date, almost no interaction between associational offices
which compile such research. Simple descriptive statistics
(median versus mean salary, for example) are measured differ-
ently from one association to another, making any universal
observations, even about librarians in associations (as
opposed to all librarians), difficult. Any association study
is marred by the fact that individuals who have decided to af-
filiate with a professional association which represents their
area of specialization have separated themselves from librarians in general and thus may be more motivated. Though some
studies take into account larger samples, they have been
few.[3]

American Library Association

The American Library Association (ALA) conducted a salary survey in 1970 which also provided some very broad indications of type of positions held and sexual makeup of the membership (Manchak, 1971). Such work is of great importance since it provides a standard and a measure against which new findings may be discussed. The preliminary report of the COSWL study used the 1970 survey to provide comparative information on status gains by ALA members in the seventies (Estabrook and Heim, 1980).

American Society for Information Science

The American Society for Information Science (ASIS) membership profile issued in 1980 was released after the COSWL study (King et al., 1980). Its analysis, however, will be helpful as the analysis of COSWL data continues. ASIS members exhibit the same general traits as those of ALA members: women function supportively and earn less than men who administer and earn more. Median information allows comparison on some traits.

Special Libraries Association

The Special Libraries Association (SLA) has executed the most comprehensive longitudinal membership survey of all the major professional library associations (SLA, 1970, 1973, 1976, 1979, 1980). While salary is the primary focus of these studies other variables, such as supervisory responsibility, are included in one or more of the SLA reports.

Society of American Archivists

The Society of American Archivists (SAA) studies confirmed similar trends in the archival profession (Deutrich, 1973; Ad Hoc Committee on the Status of Women in the Archival Profession, Society of American Archivists, 1974; Deutrich and DeWhitt, 1980; Deutrich, 1981). Salaries of women were lower than those of men. Experience and type of employment did not totally explain the differences in salary.

American Association of Law Librarians

The annual American Association of Law Librarians (AALL) survey does not include salary data by sex. Information on salary and compensation differences between male and female librarians, however, is available in separate studies at the national level using the AALL membership as a base (Frarey, 1970; Hughes, 1971; Renshawe, 1976) as well as in a number of regional or local studies (Shediac, 1978; Estes, 1979; Shediac, 1980; Leinbach and Beardwood, 1980). Salary is the primary variable analyzed by sex. In all cases women in legal settings earn less than men.

Music Library Association

No recent studies have examined the differences in professional status between male and female members of the Music Library Association (MLA). Studies done in 1969 (Filter, 1969; Filter and Marco, 1970) did identify a salary difference in favor of men as well as indications that men were more active professionally than women members.

Association for Educational Communications and Technology

In an attempt to gain a better understanding of the school media field, one survey of the membership of the Association for Educational Communications and Technology (AECT) was examined which included analysis of several variables by sex (Molenda and Cambre, March, 1977; April, 1977). This survey found that women earn less than men, and the authors observe that this may be because of the concentration of women AECT members in library settings while men tended to hold jobs in the communications industry or media centers.

TYPE OF LIBRARY STUDIES

To determine what kinds of variables would provide a basis of comparison, general studies of different library types were examined in addition to studies conducted using library associations as the sampling base. These are discussed by library type.

Academic Libraries

The best longitudinal statistical data categorized by sex for academic libraries appears in the annual salary reports of the Association of Research Libraries, the ARL Salary Survey (Frankie, 1977, 1978; Fretwell, February 1980, December 1980). In these most scholarly and prestigious libraries the most striking disparity in the difference in treatment between men's and women's administrative achievements was evident. The 1980 survey showed that 84.7% of the directors were male with an average salary of $48,084 compared to $44,871 for females. Regardless of experience, males in ARL libraries earned more than females except as head of Documents/Maps and Circulation.

Head librarians in academic institutions are compared with 51 other top administrators in the surveys conducted by the College and University Personnel Association (CUPA) and in 1976 a report was prepared on the women and minorities represented (Van Alstyne et al., 1977). This report corroborates the inequity between male and female librarians and also demonstrates the relative financial status of library administrators among higher education administrators.

The most recent ALA Association of College and Research Li-

braries salary survey (which collected data from all academic
libraries not just ACRL members) was conducted in 1976 (Talbot
and von der Lippe) and linked to earlier Council on Library
Resources (Cameron and Heim, 1970, 1972, 1974) and the
American Association of University Professors faculty compensation surveys ("Two Steps Backward," 1975). The ALA/ACRL
survey provided a great deal of information on the comparative
status of men and women in academic settings including sexual
distribution by job, salary comparisons at all job levels, minority distribution and comparisons of this information in
four types of academic libraries: universities, five-year institutions, four-year colleges, and two-year colleges.
   The ALA Office for Library Personnel Resources affirmative
action study (ALA/OLPR, 1981) provides general demographic and
salary data on race, ethnicity, origin, and sex of academic
librarians at large and for director, head of department, and
beginning positions.

Public Libraries

   Longitudinal data on public library directors serving popu-
lations of 100,000 or more have been compiled in a Library
Journal series since 1972 (Carpenter and Shearer, 1972, 1974,
1976; Heim and Kacena, 1979, 1980). These analyses demon-
strate the tendency of women to head smaller libraries, earn a
lower median salary, generate less funding, and command less
pay for beginning librarians than male directors in the same
sample. The LJ series provides comparisons for geographical
regions as well as Canada. Comparison with other municipal
administrators is possible through examination of data in the
Municipal Yearbook (Wolfson, 1980).
   Government information on public library personnel lags behind current practice. A report released in 1980 compares the
relative proportion of men and women working in public libraries by size of population served (U.S. Office of Education, 1980). This report indicates that the larger the
library, the greater the percentage of men on the staff. The
ALA/OLPR (1981) study cited above for academic librarians also
provides salary, racial, ethnic, and sex information for all
professional public library employees at large as well as discrete information at the director, branch head and beginning
levels.

School Libraries

   No major studies have compared male and female librarians
employed in school settings. Comprehensive salary information, which provides scheduled salary means and paid salary
means for professionals as well as salaries paid to library
assistants, is available from Educational Research Services.
Comparative data for classroom teachers and other professionals is included (Educational Research Services, Inc., 1980).

State Libraries and Agencies

Librarians employed in state libraries and state library agencies are examined in Survey of State Library Agencies, 1977 (Wilkins, 1979) which found a greater proportion of management positions held by men. The American Library Association/Association of Specialized Cooperative Library Agencies also supplies salary information, undifferentiated by sex, for eight state library positions (ALA/ASCLA, 1980). Salary data, not categorized by sex, appear in the annual salary surveys issued by the U.S. Office of Personnel Management (1973-) and can be compared to the earnings of other state officials.

Library of Congress

The Women's Program at the Library of Congress monitors the status of women at LC. Information on the percentage of women at various management levels is provided as well as the status of minority women ("Women's Program," 1979, 1980, 1981).

Library School Faculty

Since 1976 data about library science faculty have been analyzed by sex (Bidlack, 1976, 1977, 1978, 1979, 1980). These annual surveys state that approximately 80% of the dean and director positions are held by men and that their salaries are consistently higher than those of their female counterparts. The higher academic ranks are held by men, but women are equally represented in the lower teaching ranks. Another study by Bidlack (March 14, 1979) assessed the future availability of women and minorities for library education positions by analyzing the pool of doctoral students for an affirmative action study.

Medical Libraries

Two major studies of librarians in large biomedical libraries (Goldstein and Hill, 1975, 1980) found a striking disproportion in the number of women in the overall health sciences librarian work force compared to women holding director positions. The number of women in top posts has declined since the early fifties. Medical school libraries displayed similar characteristics in a 1976-77 study (Stangl and Hoke, 1977) which found that women in medical school libraries earn a median salary nearly $4,000 less than that earned by men.

Other Information Professionals

As noted earlier, the library science field expands daily. Scattered information from the frontiers of librarianship contributed to an overall understanding of these new areas of the library work force. Salary data in Online ("Salary and Budget Survey," 1979), The Information Manager ("Aim Profiles," 1980), Datamation (Shaw, 1980), and Computer Careers News

("Recruiter Surveys," 1981) provided a broader background for
undertaking salary analysis but little sex differentiated data.

LIBRARY SUMMARY: CONCLUSION

Analysis of the surveys which examined the status of new
graduates, librarians in associations, and the professional
staff of different types of libraries identified the various
areas to be considered in the design of the survey for the
sample of ALA membership used in the present study. This was
done so that the findings of this survey could be compared to
those of other studies.[4] This analysis also indicated the
need for standardization in this variety of studies. While
the present study focuses on ALA members only, library work
force analysts should attempt to generate other data with more
standardization so that surveys can be compared.

2 Methodology of the COSWL Study

SAMPLING

A seven-page questionnaire was distributed to a random sample of 3,000 personal members of the American Library Association. Lay, student and trustee members were excluded from the sample, but retirees were not. Such a large sample was necessary because of the small percentage of men within the profession and the distribution of members into a variety of different types of library positions. The large sample allowed analysis of data by type of library and strengthened the validity of the inferences drawn about the differences in treatment between men and women within the association. The questionnaire was pretested on a random sample of 50 ALA members in January 1980. It was then revised and sent to the sample of 3,000 in March 1980. The March mailing included a copy of the questionnaire, a stamped return envelope, and a stamped return postcard that the respondent could use to indicate that the questionnaire had been returned. The questionnaires themselves were not coded in any way to reveal the identity of the respondent because of the personal nature of a number of questions. Those who did not return the postcard within five weeks received a follow-up postcard reminder. Unfortunately, budgetary constraints prevented any further follow-up to individuals who did not respond to the mailing.

From these two mailings 1,987 usable responses were received. Twenty-nine others had to be discarded because of lack of information, incorrect addresses, or death of the respondent. The response rate for the study was 67.1 percent.

10

QUESTIONNAIRE DESIGN

As indicated above, previous research on women's career development was an important determinant of the types of questions asked in the COSWL study. From available evidence, it seems that a number of variables affect the status of women within a given occupation. Moreover, status itself can be measured in a number of ways. It is not simply determined by salary. The final questionnaire asked respondents for their answers to 37 questions in the following four major areas: (1) Overall Career Pattern; (2) Current or Most Recent Job Situation; (3) Educational Background and Professional Involvement; and (4) Personal and Family Data.

Overall Career Pattern

Respondents were asked to provide information on career history. Although the data represent ALA members at one specific time, respondents were asked for a summary of individual career histories including type of organization, job title, dates held, and whether the job was full- or part-time. Respondents were also asked to indicate what their general career pattern had been. A number of studies focusing on either women or men and women provided background and validation for development of this section.

The complexity of women's career patterns is outlined in Life Styles of Educated Women (Ginzberg, 1966), which notes that for men career problems take center stage, and only incidental attention need be given their lives off the job, but women's careers interact significantly with other facets of their lives. Ginzberg identified the following four lifestyles followed by the women he studied in 1963: (1) individualistic--a striving after autonomy; (2) influential--a drive to influence people and events; (3) supportive; and (4) communal. An update to Ginzberg's work by one of his associates, Alice M. Yohalem, takes into account the women's movement and new social elements (Yohalem, 1979). Eichler (1975) noted the need to establish women's work patterns on their own terms rather than as deviant from men's. Work discontinuity was examined by Corcoran and Duncan (1979) who found that even with controls for this possibility, white men earned substantially more than most women. Rossi (1965) suggested the following three patterns for women: homemakers, pioneers (women in male-dominated fields), and traditionals. Simpson and Simpson (1969) examined discontinuity in the work of librarians.

Angrist (1972) pointed out the need to view women's career aspirations as integral to life-style choices since studying choice of occupation alone obliterates the complexity of women's realistic attempts to anticipate and juggle their many roles. Very little evidence that career-salient women are

committed to choosing a total lifestyle rather than an occupation emerged from this study.

Levitt's study (1971) of career patterns of librarians assigned subjects to four categories, modifying Super's (1957)
and Mulvey's (1963) research on career patterns of women. The
four categories included the following: Stable Working Career
Pattern; Double Track Career Pattern; Interrupted Career Pattern and Delayed Entrance Career Pattern. Specific general
studies of librarians' career patterns included Taylor's study
(1973) of mobility characteristics, Edsall's (1973) composite
picture of career patterns of community college librarians;
and Rhodes's analysis (1975) of black female librarians.

Other professional groups have been studied. A number of
these studies provided background. These studies include data
on general career patterns of black women administrators in
colleges and universities (Thomas, 1976); career patterns of
women administrators in higher education (Fecher, 1972;
Gasser, 1975; and Douglas, 1976); Walsh's analysis (1975) of
California women higher-education administrators and Paul's
study (1978) of Massachusetts community college administrators. Covel (1977) and Pope (1979) examined careers of women
working as public school administrators; Cristo (1975) examined career accomplishments in the field of education.
Quadagno (1976) provided information on careers of male and
female physicians. These general studies, a small subset of
the growing literature of career patterns, supported our selection of career variables for the COSWL study. Since few
studies of librarians have included sampling across library
types and job positions, the COSWL study should stand, even
though limited to ALA members, as a major advance in the research being done on library careers.

A number of library studies which have tended to focus on
librarians in a particular setting in respect to position or
type of library were re-examined. These have been reviewed
extensively in Fennell's dissertation (1978). Items of special interest included Alvarez's study (1939) of public
library directors; Bryan's study (1952) of public libraries;
Harvey's study (1957) of chief librarians; Morrison's study
(1961) of the careers of academic librarians; Blankenship's
study (1967) of college library directors; Bradley's analysis
(1968) of succession patterns in public and academic
libraries; Schiller's various investigations (1969; 1974);
Braunagel's study (1975) of mobility as related to career
progression; Parsons' study (1976) of ARL directors; Fennell's
study (1978) of women academic library directors; Martin's
study (1978) of ARL women directors; and Dale's study of
careers of women librarians with doctorates (1980).

These earlier studies supported much of this study's questionnaire design in the career pattern area and provided
indications that both salary and status within the library

profession and other fields are higher when individuals move
between organizations rather than remain in the same one over
a long period of time. There are also indications that within
the library field, the best career path to positions adminis-
tering larger libraries is by working in technical services or
working as an administrator in a smaller library. The first
two questions of the questionnaire tested these assumptions.
The first question also provided the type of library in which
respondents worked as well as the title of the position held.

   Within the category of overall career pattern, respondents
were also asked to indicate the number of leaves taken from
the field since the time they accepted their first professional position. It has been assumed that women in the library
field more frequently take leaves and therefore fail to
achieve status equal to men who may have obtained professional
degrees at the same time.

Current or Most Recent Job Situation

   The second set of career questions to which members were
asked to respond related directly to, "job currently held"
(or, for retirees and unemployed individuals, job most recently held). These included questions on the individual's most
important reason for accepting that job, whether the individual felt over or under qualified for the position, the length
of time in that position, whether the position was classified
as full- or part-time, the extent of supervisory responsibilities, the level in the organizational hierarchy, and the
extent to which financial support or leave for research, professional activities, or continuing education was granted.
Questions about the position within the organization were
asked to provide indications of the individual's status within
the organization and were also expected to correlate with salary. The individual's reasons for accepting the position and
perceptions of the appropriateness of personal qualifications
were also expected to be salary-related in that individuals
who chose a particular job because of (for example) location
may not have been in a strong bargaining position vis-a-vis
salary. Financial and leave-time support were difficult factors to measure but seemed important, in order to examine education, professional involvement, and publications, to identify the extent to which such activities were supported by the
employing organization. Such support also seemed to provide
an indicator of possible future inequities in the achievements
of ALA members.

   Background studies used to develop and validate questions in
this section included the surveys summarized in the section
Review of the Literature (above). These studies were used to
examine various techniques by which researchers had focused on
questions of status. Stone (1969) provides a good framework
for identification of factors related to the current job situation.

In addition to library related literature, many recent studies have been conducted which examine the work place from
the point of view of women's professional positions and status. These provide some of the larger societal context
against which to gauge the place of women in library work situations. Items examined include the following: Kaufman's
thesis (1961) on the status of women in higher education administration; Bernard's volume (1964) on academic women; the
National Research Council's Office of Scientific Personnel's
first (1965) and second (1968) follow-up studies of doc-
toral-level professionals from 1935 to 1960; Leland's examination (1966) of women's career aspirations as affected by the
male environment; Hall's Occupations and the Social Structure
(1969); Epstein's paper (1970) on sex-status limits on women's
careers in the professions and her monograph (1970) on women's
options and limits in professional careers; the Professional
Women's Caucus report on women in the professions (Sixteen Reports, 1970); Oltman's American Association of University
Women report (1970) on women in higher education; Hennig's
Harvard thesis (1971) on women executives; Theodore's volume
of essays (1971) on professional women; Manhardt's examination
(1972) of male and female job orientations in business; Bose's
study (1973) on differences in occupational prestige of men
and women; Rossi and Calderwood's Russell Sage Foundation
study (1973) of academic women; Stevenson's thesis (1973) on
women administrators in Big Ten universities; the Carnegie
Commission on Higher Education's exploration (1973) of opportunities for women in higher education; Cohen's study (1975)
of women in medicine; Barron's thesis (1975) comparing characteristics of women in male and female occupations; Blaxall's
and Reagan's Signs issue (1976) on occupational segregation;
Vice's thesis (1977) on careers of women in engineering; Blau
and Hendrick's examination (1979) of occupational segregation
by sex; Rose, Menninger, and Nyre's analysis (1979) of women
in science and engineering; Buck's background paper (1979) on
the development of the Washington Assessment Center for Librarians; Osterman's case study (1979) of sex discrimination
in professional employment; and Vetter's popularized discussion (1980) on women scientists.

<u>Educational Background and Professional Involvement</u>
    This section of the questionnaire was developed in two
parts. We will discuss the background for each part separate-
ly since different literatures butressed our design and validation of questions.
    <u>Educational Background.</u> Questions on educational background
included one on formal education--degrees, dates of degrees
and dates of attendance. Respondents were also asked to indicate the type of institution they attended as an undergraduate, since there has been some evidence that women who

attend women's colleges have higher levels of achievement.
Whether or not the individual worked while studying for the
first professional degree in library science was also asked to
provide some measured socialization. No specific question
asked about mentor relationships, but it was hypothesized that
those individuals who worked within the school while studying
for the degree would have more opportunities to know faculty
well and to develop job contacts. Those who worked outside
the school in other fields and positions were hypothesized to
have the least opportunity to develop contacts.

Although vocational choice questions were outside the scope
of the COSWL study, the literature was examined for connections with educational studies. Some of these contained background information which was used. Among the most helpful
studies in the vocational choice literature were Ginzberg
et al. (1951), a classic statement of occupational choices;
Ginzberg's restatement (1972) as well as a re-analysis of his
work by Howell et al. (1977); Super's classic work on career
development and self-concept (1953, 1957, 1963); Holland's
central vocational choice monographs (1966, 1973); Almquist
and Angrist's examination (1970) of occupational choice among
college women; Yu's exploratory study (1972) of the role of
creativity in women's career choices in traditional male and
female professions; Angrist's discussion (1972) of women's
changing work aspirations during college; Osipow's reviews of
career development (1973, 1976); Sedney and Turner's test
(1975) of causal sequences in models for career orientation of
women; Valentine, Ellinger, and Williams's examination (1975)
of sex-role attitudes as they affect career choices of graduate students; the National Institute of Education, Career
Education Program report on issues of sex bias in measuring
career interest (Diamond, 1975); a synthesis of sociological
and psychological literature on educational and occupational
choice by Levine (1976) and her study of women in professional
schools (1975); Badke's dissertation (1977) on the relationship between personality needs, vocational interests, and career orientation of college women; Crawford's analysis (1978)
of career choice in pioneer and traditional women; Stake's
study (1978) of motives for occupational goal setting of
college students; and Orcutt and Walsh's study (1979) of
college women's career aspirations as they affect traditionality and congruence; and reviews of the career develop-
ment/vocational behavior literature (Betz, 1977; Holcomb and
Anderson, 1977; Zytowski, 1978; and Walsh et al., 1979).
Three examinations of the library profession as a career
choice (Reagan, 1958; Reeling, 1965; Magrill, 1969) provided
specific investigations into this area.

Most of the studies which dealt with careers in general (as
reviewed above) included information on educational background. Additional helpful studies included the following:

Letarte's dissertation (1968) on the effect of formal study and work experience on occupational and self-concepts of librarians; Astin's Russell Sage report (1969) on the women doctorate; Centra's study (1974) Women, Men and the Doctorate; Bob's study (1977) on differences in financial aid for male and female students; Sukiennik's dissertation (1978) on training women library school students for greater career achievement; the National Center for Education Statistics report Degree Awards to Women (Brown, 1979); and Dale's examination (1980) of women librarians holding the doctorate.

Professional Involvement. As Stone (1969) has discussed at length, there are many variables by which professional involvement may be measured. The questionnaire for the present study focused on two primary areas: association activities and research and publication.

The relationship of status to professional involvement was explored by requesting information on state and national association responsibilities at three levels: as elected officer or representative; as chair of a committee, section or division; and as a member of a committee, section, or division. Research and publication activities were investigated by offering respondents a variety of forms of publications to checkoff (author of book; editor or compiler of book or journal; journal or periodical author; technical paper; paper presented at conference; paper published in conference proceedings; research completed but manuscript unpublished; and book reviews). For each category respondents were requested to indicate the number of each of publications.

There is a growing body of sociological literature which guided the inquiries in this area. A central piece was Simon, Clark and Galway's comparison (1967) of the productivity of men and women professors as measured by publications and professional recognition. Other generally important items included the following: Epstein's discussion (1970) on limits in women's professional careers and Freeman's remarks (1977) on faculty women in American universities. Items from the library literature included Bloomfield's essay (1966) on the writing habits of librarians; Watson (1977) on the publication activity of academic librarians; O'Connor and Van Orden (1978) on "getting into print"; Olsgaard and Olsgaard (1980) on authorship in library periodicals; and Rayman and Goudy's analysis (1980) of research and publication requirements in university libraries.

Professional association involvement was studied in depth for the period from 1876 to 1921 (Corwin, 1974) but no updates to her study have been conducted. COSWL findings on the disproportionate percentages of women involved in professional organizations and in publication indicated that the profession has far to go to achieve parity in these areas.

Personal and Family Data

Any study which seeks to find differences in the professional treatment of men and women must gather substantial personal
data against which to measure other types of information.
Questions about age, sex, family status, mobility, race, individual and family income, family responsibilities, parental
and spouse education and employment, and family environment
were asked. Most of the studies cited above included some
sort of demographic data gathering. Since the COSWL study was
interested in women's careers particularly, the growing amount
of literature concerning the effect of child and family care
on careers, problems of dual careers, and questions of mobility was reviewed.

Sexual data on librarians have been discussed and documented
rather extensively in the library literature (Weibel and Heim,
1979) and form the basis, in fact, for the COSWL study investigation. More extensive racial data are beginning to be
compiled. In addition to studies on new graduates (American
Library Association Office for Library Personnel Resources,
n.d. and 1980) which explore the racial, sexual, and ethnic
makeup of new entrants to the profession, ALA/OLPR (1981) has
completed an affirmative action study which examines the
information above for academic and public libraries, allowing
a larger framework for the discussion of these connections in
the COSWL data. The initial report on the COSWL data
(Estabrook and Heim, 1980) explores the racial makeup of ALA.

Marital status is an important aspect of this study since it
has been hypothesized that married women experience mobility
problems and that this may account for the general depressed
status of women in the profession. In addition to mobility
studies by Taylor (1973) and Braunagel (1975, 1979) which focused on librarians specifically, the following works were examined: Cristo's dissertation (1975) on women in education
and factors influencing career mobility; Niemi's essay (1975)
on geographic immobility and labor force mobility; Miller's
examination (1976) on the affect of the family life cycle, extended family orientation, and economic aspirations on mobility; the Institute for Research on Poverty discussion paper
(Marwell, 1976) on residence location, geographic mobility and
academic women; and Curby's dissertation (1978) on the geographic mobility of women in higher education administrative
posts.

Also considered was the burgeoning literature on dual careers. This has been summarized in the recent Catalyst bibliography (1980). Of special help were the following: the
early report by Weil (1961) on factors influencing married
women's participation in the labor force; Rubin's article
(1968) on hypergamy; Rapoport and Rapoport (1969) on the dual
career family and a later study (1971); Holmstrom's dissertation (1970) on intertwining career patterns of husbands and

wives and her monograph (1972) on the two-career family;
Levitt's dissertation (1971) on career patterns and life history characteristics; Sussman and Cogswell's essay (1971) on
family influence on job movement; Hall and Gordon (1973) on
career choices of married women; Long's study (1974) of family
residential mobility and women's labor force participation;
Glen et al. (1974) on patterns of intergenerational mobility
of females through marriage; Hall's study (1975) of work, personal, and home pressures on married women; Wolf's dissertation (1975) on the occupational achievements of married women;
Burke and Weir's discussion (1976) of personality differences
between members of one- and two-career families; Duncan and
Perrucci (1976) on dual occupation families and migration;
Hunt and Hunt's essay (1977) in <u>Social Problems</u> on dilemmas
and contradictions of status for dual-career families; Huser
and Grant (1978) on differences between husbands and wives in
traditional and dual-career families; an examination of status
benefits derived from working wives in the <u>Journal of Marriage
and the Family</u> (Hiller and Philliber, 1978); Perrucci and
Taorg (1978) on work commitment among married women college
graduates; the constraints on women's employment because of
husband's occupation (Mortimer, Hall, and Reuben, 1978);
Middleton's report (1979) in <u>The Chronicle of Higher Education</u>
that marriage curbs women's careers in academe; and Maynard
and Zawacki (1979) on mobility and the dual-career couple.
The collection of salary-related data was done in the context
of the many studies of librarians' salaries which are reviewed
above in connection with general surveys of the library work
force. These are also reviewed for the period of the seventies with comparative tabular data by Heim (1982).

Information on family responsibilities was asked in order to
develop a framework for comparison of men's and women's total
workloads. There was very little investigation of this issue
in the library literature. Sociological studies which helped
to formulate questions included: Anshen's early monograph
(1949) <u>The Family: Its Functions and Destiny</u>; Nagely (1971)
on traditional and pioneer working mothers; Etaugh's study
(1974) of the effects of maternal employment on children;
Hoffman and Nye's monograph (1975) evaluating the consequences
of being a working mother for the wife, husband, and child;
Sawhill's essay (1976) on discrimination and poverty among
women who head families; Altman (1977) on the career plans of
women and maternal employment; Hamovitch and Morgenstern
(1977) on the productivity of academic women with children;
and Beckman's paper (1978) in the <u>Psychology of Women
Quarterly</u> on the relative rewards and costs of parenthood for
employed women.

Family background information was explored in several library science studies (among others, Rhodes, 1975; Fennell,
1978). Other items which supported the development of these

questions included Toman's monograph (1969), <u>Family Constel-</u><u>lation--Its Effects on Personality and Social Behavior</u>; Sewell et al. (1970) on the educational and early occupational status attainment process; Regan's dissertation (1972) on the achievement of freshmen women in relation to their mothers' career patterns; Patrick's dissertation (1973) on the family background of women who enter the male-dominated professions; Stein and Bailey (1973) on the socialization of achievement orientation in females; Goodale and Hall (1976) on the influence of sex, parents, and values on career selection; Jarman's dissertation (1976) on the effect of parental messages on the career patterns of professional women; Safilios-Rothchild (1976) on connections between the occupational and family systems; Ritchie and Boehm (1977) on biographical data as a predictor of women's and men's potential for management; Scheresky (1977) on occupational sex-typing in young children; Rosenfeld (1978) on maternal employment and socio-economic status as factors in the creativity of daughters' career choices.

Items on the relationship of spouse's occupation and education tended to be the same items discussed above in connection with marital status.

Since birth order has been studied (Altus, 1966; Bayer, 1967) as a factor in achievement, information was also requested on the family size and place of respondents in the sibling order.

The foregoing review of the literature that was used to develop the COSWL questionnaire should direct researchers wishing to understand the intellectual framework which undergirded the preparations to gather career and personal information on librarians. An analysis of the COSWL data follows.

3 Analysis of Major Findings

The COSWL study contained a sample of personal members of
the American Library Association and included both active and
retired individuals. Of the 1,987 respondents, 86.6%
(n=1,714) are employed, 4.6% (n=91) are unemployed but considered active, and 8.8% (n=174) are retired. The status of
eight of the members could not be determined. It should be
noted that a number of individuals who indicated that they are
retired have re-entered the labor force, some in volunteer and
others in paid positions. The first section of the analysis
examines responses from the total sample of personal members
who responded to the COSWL questionnaire. The major portion
of the analysis, however, focuses on those individuals who reported that they are currently (as of the 1980 date of the
study) employed full-time. This allows meaningful comparisons
with regard to salary and employment of ALA members and also
some analysis of the way in which ALA members compare to other
professional membership groups that have been studied.

PERSONAL MEMBERS OF ALA

Members of the association are predominantly female and predominantly white. Females make up 78.3% (n=1,552) of the membership; men, 21.7% (n=435). A racial breakdown of the
membership reveals that 94% (n=1,847) are white; 3.1% (n=61)
are black; and the remaining 2.9% (n=79) include American In-
dians, Asian Americans, and individuals from other identified
minority groups. The median age of members of the American
Library Association is 44.7 years.
A majority of the personal members, 54.5% (n=1,080), report
being married; 29.7% (n=588) have never been married; 13.4%

(n=265) are divorced, separated, or widowed; and 2.3% (n=45) are part of a committed, long-term relationship. This last category was included in the questionnaire because it was felt that such relationships may affect both the mobility and financial opportunities of individuals in much the same way that marriage might and therefore could be expected to have some bearing on the respondent's career. In response to a question about children and family obligations, 44.9% (n=892) of the ALA members indicated that they had children for whom they were responsible and 15.1% (n=297) had responsibility for other dependents (e.g., parents) during some time in their career.

The educational level of members is as was expected; less than 2% (1.7%, n=34) report not having the baccalaureate degree. The master's degree in library science is held by 93.1% (n=1,765) of the members. Advanced work beyond the master's has been pursued by 10.5% (n=208) of the respondents with 7% (n=137) having received a doctorate (Ph.D., D.L.S., or Ed.D.).

Of those individuals in the study who acquired the professional degree, 61.8% (n=1,180) worked during their professional program. Approximately half of those working were employed within their library school (a total of 30.5%, n=552, of the group sampled). Awards were received by 35.8% (n=675) of the members during their professional education.

Information on the careers of these members indicates that as a group they have been highly mobile and active within the profession. Only 10.6% (n=205) report having spent their careers in the same position within the same organization. This contrasts to the 45.1% (n=873) who have worked in different positions within different organizations and an additional 19.5% (n=378) who have worked in similar positions but in different organizations. Although less than 20% (18.8%, n=370) report having been elected or appointed to a national position, fully 46.5% (n=912) have been members of a committee of a national professional association. ALA members have been even more active on the state or regional level with 42.1% (n=828) reporting election or appointment to an office at that level and 62.2% (n=1,226) indicating that they have been members of state or regional committees.

The COSWL questionnaire asked a number of questions about publishing activities of ALA members. Book authorship was claimed by 8.3% (n=165) of the respondents. Thirty percent (n=602) indicate that they have written a journal article. This is a slightly higher percentage than found for members writing book reviews (22.3%, n=443).

This general profile of ALA members is not surprising to those who are active in the profession and who attend meetings of the association. It portrays a group that is predominantly white, female, and middle-aged. The findings that are less visible are the levels of professional training and activity

of ALA members. As a group, it is a highly educated population. Members appear to have been involved actively in the
field since the time of their professional training. They
have worked in a variety of situations, and a significant percentage of the members have contributed to the research and
association activities of the profession.

MEMBERS EMPLOYED FULL-TIME

   Of the 1,987 respondents to the COSWL study, 1,580 indicated
that they are currently employed full-time. Of these, 1,199
(75.9%) are female and 381 (24.1%) are male. The following
analysis examines the personal, career, professional, and employment characteristics of this group with specific attention
to differences in professional status between female and male
members of the American Library Association. Following a descriptive analysis of these differences, a report of results
of multivariate analyses which sought to determine the extent
to which sex and other factors contribute to established differences within the profession will follow. It should be
noted briefly that the total number of respondents in each
category does not always equal 1,580 because of the absence of
responses to some items on the questionnaire.

Personal Characteristics by Gender
   As noted above, 1,199 members of the employed members are
female, representing 75.9% of the sample. This represents a
somewhat lower percentage than that of females in the total
membership--a reflection of the different mortality rates of
men and women, an increased likelihood that women are working
part-time or are unemployed, and possibly a slight shift in
the proportion of men and women entering the field of librarianship (although data of the present study and that of
other studies do not clearly indicate such a trend). There
were 381 men (24.1%) who indicated that they are employed
full-time. A racial breakdown of each group (table 1) indicates that 93.7% of the women are white as are 93.6% of the
men. The only other racial groups represented in significant
number are black Americans who make up 3.9% of the female ALA
membership and 1.6% of the males, and Puerto Ricans. Eleven
men (2.9%) in the sample identified themselves as Puerto Rican.

Table 1.   Racial Composition of Employed Membership by Sex

| | Female | | Male | |
	%	N	%	N
Asian American	1.6	19	0.8	3
Puerto Rican	0.3	3	2.9	11
Spanish surname	0.2	2	0.5	2
White	93.7	1115	93.6	350
Black	3.9	46	1.6	6
Mexican American	0.1	1	0.0	0
Other/mixed	0.3	4	0.5	2
TOTAL	100.1*	1190	99.0*	374

x^2 = 18.6; p < .01 with 7 d.f.

*Do not equal 100% due to rounding

Questions on the marital and family status of ALA members revealed that women are less likely to be married or involved in long-term relationships than men (table 2) and, correspondingly, fewer women indicated that they have children for whom they have or have had responsibility. Less than half (48.9%) of the women are married and another 2.6% indicate they are part of a committed long-term relationship. Sixty-six percent of the men are married and 3.2% have long-term relationships. Fifteen percent more of the men (55.6%, n=212) have children than the women (40.4%, n=484). A slightly higher proportion of men (16.4%, n=62) than women (12.3%, n=146) also indicated that they had had responsibility for dependents during their professional career.

Despite the greater responsibilities of men, almost twice as many women as men indicated that they had limits to their mobility. When asked whether there are any personal or familial responsibilities that limit their mobility in job seeking, 57.3% of the women (n=680) said yes compared to only 33.5% (n=126) of the men.

Table 2.   Family Status of ALA Members by Sex

| | Female | | Male | |
	%	N	%	N
Married	48.9	584	66.0	250
Long term relationship	2.6	31	3.2	12
Divorced, separated, widowed	16.2	194	7.1	27
Never married	32.3	386	23.7	90
TOTAL	100.0	1195	100.0	379

x^2 = 40.2; p = .00 with 3 d.f.

Respondents were asked to provide information on the education and occupation of parents and spouse (table 3). Educational levels were coded in accordance with the categories listed in table 3; thus the discussion of mean educational level should be examined with reference to that table. For example, a group mean educational level of 2.5 indicates that, on the average, that group achieved an educational level between high school graduation and some college. An examination of the mean educational level of parents and spouse of ALA members indicates that women in the association come from a family background in which the educational level of both mother and father is higher than that of either the father or

Table 3. Education of Parents and Spouse by Sex

	Female		Male	
	%	N	%	N
Father				
no high school	26.7	316	36.9	138
high school grad	22.0	260	26.2	98
some college	18.0	213	11.2	42
college grad	13.8	163	10.4	39
graduate work	4.7	56	3.7	14
graduate degree	14.7	174	11.5	43
TOTAL	99.9*	1182	99.9*	374
mean	2.92		2.52	

$x^2 = 26.11$; $p = .00$ with 6 d.f.

Mother's education				
no high school	22.0	259	30.3	114
high school grad	31.7	374	33.5	126
some college	20.6	243	15.4	58
college grad	15.9	188	14.1	53
graduate work	4.4	52	1.9	7
graduate degree	5.3	63	4.8	18
TOTAL	100.0*	1179	100.0*	376
mean	2.65		2.38	

$x^2 = 18.34$; $p = .005$ with 6 d.f.

Spouse's education				
mean	4.90		5.72	

$x^2 = 39.42$; $p = .00$ with 6 d.f.

*Does not equal 100% due to rounding

mother of male members of the association. The mean educational level of fathers of women is 2.9 and for mothers it is 2.6. For the men in the study, mean educational level of fathers is 2.5 and for mothers it is 2.4. This seems to confirm other research which has suggested that professions such as teaching and librarianship provide an opportunity for upward mobility for men of lower socio-economic status. It has been suggested that as opportunities for women in law, business, and medicine become open, women of higher status will enter these areas rather than those traditionally open to them.

In contrast to this are the data on spouses' education. The men are marrying up; the women, down. Mean educational level for wives of ALA men is 5.7. For husbands of women in the association it is 4.9.

PROFESSIONAL PREPARATION

Preparation for the profession was assessed through a series of questions on ALA members' formal education since high school, their reasons for selecting a particular professional school, and whether they received awards and/or worked during their professional training.

Almost all employed members surveyed indicated that they hold the baccalaureate degree. Only 16 (1.4%) of the women and 3 (0.8%) of the men have not completed that degree. The fields in which members majored are slightly more concentrated for women than for men. Over 60% (62.8%, n=750) of the women report receiving their degree in one of the following five areas: English (26.1%, n=312); history (12.1%, n=144); education (12.9%, n=154); modern languages (5.8%, n=69); and library science (5.9%, n=71). In contrast, only the following three areas were reported as concentrations by over 5% of the men: English (22.3%, n=84); history (21.0%, n=79); and arts/humanities (5.1%, n=19). The median date for receipt of the baccalaureate is 1964 for women and 1961 for men.

Advanced degrees of all types are held by a higher proportion of men than women in the COSWL study. The MLS is held by 90.3% (n=344) of the men and 86.9% (n=1,042) of the women. At the post-master's level, 23.2% (n=90) of the men report receiving a degree and fully 16.1% (n=61) of the men sampled indicated that they hold the doctoral degree. In contrast, only 8% (n=100) of the women have a post-master's degree. The doctorate is held by 2.5% (n=30). In absolute numbers, twice as many men as women report receiving the doctoral degree.

There are also significant differences between the experiences of male and female members of the association during the period of their library education (table 4).

Table 4. Library School Experience of Full-Time Employed
          ALA Members by Sex

	Female		Male	
	%	N	%	N
Worked during the MLS				
No	38.5	425	28.2	97
Yes, within school	30.2	334	37.2	128
Yes, outside in library	24.8	274	25.0	86
Yes, in other field	6.5	72	9.6	33
TOTAL	100.0	1105	100.0	344

$x^2 = 15.1$; p = .00 with 3 d.f.

	Female		Male	
	%	N	%	N
Awards during the MLS				
No	63.1	725	59.5	219
Yes	36.9	424	40.5	149
TOTAL	100.0	1149	100.0	368

$x^2 = 1.4$; p = .24 with 1 d.f.

Men were more likely to have worked in situations that would
give them access to future job opportunities, e.g., within the
library school. Of the full-time employed women in the sample, 30.2% (n=334) worked within the school compared to 37.2%
(n=128) of the men. Men were also more likely to have obtained work experience of some form during their professional
education with 72.8% (n=247) of the men reporting having
worked during the MLS. Ten percent fewer of the women respondents (62.5%, n=680) worked at that time. By a slightly
higher margin (3.6%), men in the sample were also more likely
to have received some award during their work on the MLS. Of
the women in the sample, 36.9% (n=424) received an award while
working for the professional degree. This compares to 40.5%
(n=149) of the men who report receiving awards. The difference is not statistically significant.
    There were no significant differences, either, between men
and women in their reasons for selecting a particular professional school (table 5).

Table 5. Priorities for Choosing a Professional School by Sex

	Female		Male	
	%	N	%	N
Location	52.0	558	51.5	183
Reputation	23.1	248	24.5	87
Program	14.2	152	11.6	41
Faculty	0.7	8	1.7	6
Other	10.0	107	10.7	38
TOTAL	100.0	1073	100.0	355

$x^2 = 4.1$; p = .39 with 4 d.f.

These findings with regard to the professional education of
members of the American Library Association indicate that men
have the advantage of greater access to the library community
during their education and to rewards from their schools. Men
also are more likely to hold professional credentials that may
be a prerequisite for some of the more prestigious and more
lucrative positions within the library field.

CAREER PATTERNS OF ALA MEMBERS

Two questions were asked of participants in the COSWL study
to obtain information on their overall career patterns.
First, respondents were asked to indicate whether they had
worked in similar or different positions in similar or different organizations. Second, they were asked whether they
had had any career interruptions and, if so, for what reasons
and for what length of time.
The overall career patterns of ALA members are relatively
similar for men and women (table 6). A slightly higher percentage of women than men indicate that they have worked in
similar positions within different organizations. A higher
proportion of men than women indicate that they have worked in
different positions within different organizations throughout
their careers. This may be a possible contributor to getting
administrative positions since job mobility is often seen to
be related to opportunities for promotion.

Table 6. Overall Career Pattern of ALA Members by Sex

	Female		Male	
	%	N	%	N
Same position/same organization	10.7	126	9.3	35
Similar positions/same organization	8.9	104	6.1	23
Different positions/ different organization	17.3	203	16.8	63
Similar positions/ different organization	20.0	235	16.8	63
Different positions/ different organization	43.1	505	51.1	192
TOTAL	100.00	1173	100.2*	376

$$x^2 = 9.2; p = .10 \text{ with } 5 \text{ d.f.}$$

*Does not equal 100% due to rounding

Career interruptions were experienced more frequently by
women than men with 29.4% (n=351) of the women reporting at
least one career interruption compared to 22.6% (n=86) of the
men. For both men and women who have taken leave, the median
length of time spent out of the library profession is the
same: 1.8 years. The reasons for leaving the field differ,
however, with men most frequently citing education (50%, n=43)
and military service (20.2%, n=18) and women mentioning educational reasons (37.6%, n=132), pregnancy or childcare
(29.2%, n=109) or moving (23%, n=84).

EMPLOYMENT CHARACTERISTICS OF CURRENT JOBS

An examination of employment characteristics of jobs
currently held by ALA members reveals even more substantial
differences in professional status between male and female librarians. The factors that were analyzed included salary,
type of organization and position, highest priority for
accepting the position, level in the organizational hierarchy,
supervisory responsibility, and financial and other types of
support for professional activities.
The COSWL findings confirmed those of other studies with regard to salary differences between men and women in the profession. Questions were asked about both individual and total
family income since the level of family resources was seen to
be one indicator of an individual's ability to purchase childcare, household help, professional travel or other unreim-
bursed expenses that might contribute to an individual's
career development. Total family income also provides a way
of including consulting and other income additional to salary. Women lag far behind men in both base salary and total
family income. Median salary for women (as of the 1979 calendar year) was $14,700. For men the median was $19,500.
Median total family income for women was $23,700. The compar-
able figure for men was $26,100. One possible explanation for
the difference in total family income of men and women is the
difference in marital status of the two groups. It may also
be explained in part by the differences found in the relative
status of the spouses of the two groups. Another important
explanation is the difference in types of jobs held and level
of responsibility assigned.

JOB CLASSIFICATION

Women and men members of ALA are represented in different
proportions in the different types of library organizations
(table 7). Almost half (46.2%, n=174) of the men are employed
in academic libraries compared to 29.6% (n=349) of the women.

In contrast, only 3.4% (n=13) of the men report working in any
type of school library, an organization in which 17% (n=200)
of the women in the sample are employed.

Table 7. Current Place of Employment by Sex

	Female		Male	
	%	N	%	N
Academic library	29.6	349	46.2	174
Public library	30.8	363	22.8	86
School	17.0	200	3.4	13
Special	6.5	77	6.6	25
Library education	1.9	22	5.6	21
Other (includes systems, consultants, and organizations other than libraries)	14.2	168	15.4	58
TOTAL	100.0	1179	100.0	377

Women are also represented in greater numbers in public libraries with 30.8% (n=363) of the women in the sample compared
to 22.8% (n=86) of the men indicating that they are affiliated
with public libraries.

Although the number of men and women working in library education is approximately the same (22 women and 21 men), proportionally 5.6% of the men compared to 1.9% of the women are
library school faculty.

We have included the number of individuals working in special libraries also; but suspect that inferences from these
data to the total population of special librarians may be of
limited validity. ALA does not seem to be the primary professional association for individuals in these types of organizations.

Data from the COSWL study also support other studies with
regard to differences between women and men in the types of
positions held within their organizations: a much lower percentage of women hold high level administrative positions.
This can be seen if one examines occupational title (table 8)
and level in the organizational hierarchy (table 9) of members
of the association.

Table 8. Occupational Title by Sex

	Female		Male	
	%	N	%	N
Librarian, general	26.9	319	14.9	56
Professor	3.5	42	8.0	30
Library director	10.1	120	24.4	92
Assistant/associate director	3.8	45	8.2	31
Public service, head	3.7	44	2.1	8
Technical service, head	4.0	48	4.0	15
Public service, other	11.8	140	6.9	26
Technical service, other	6.2	73	6.9	26
Media specialist	5.4	64	1.9	7
Children's librarian	3.2	38	0.3	1
Department head	8.7	103	10.9	41
Librarian, other	2.0	24	0.8	3
Other	10.6	126	10.9	41
TOTAL	99.9*	1186	100.2*	377

x^2 = 180.9; p = .00 with 51 d.f.

*Does not equal 100% due to rounding

If we isolate the director, assistant/associate director, and department and area administrators, 49.6% (n=187) of the men can be categorized as administrators. This compares to only 30.4% (n=360) of the women in similar positions.

It could be argued that lack of precision in job titles within organizations make these data suspect. Further evidence of women's lower status in administration is provided from data on supervisory responsibility and organizational position.

Men and women in the COSWL study work in organizations of similar size. For both, the median number of employees in the organization is 49.7. Men, however, have greater supervisory responsibility and are likely to be higher in the organizational hierarchy. The median number of professionals supervised by men is 3.7; for women, it is 1.1. The median number of nonprofessionals supervised by men is 4.5; by women, 2.4. Women have not been in their organizations as long as the men (a median of six years for women vs. seven years for men in the study). This is one possible contributing factor to the different levels of responsibility. Women also indicated somewhat different priorities for accepting their most recent job (table 9).

Table 9. Highest Priority for Accepting Most Recent Job by Sex

	Female		Male	
	%	N	%	N
Status	5.0	55	10.0	36
Salary	6.4	71	10.0	36
Challenge	41.8	462	39.0	140
Location	22.2	245	10.0	36
Advancement	7.4	82	11.4	41
Personal/family	0.9	10	1.9	7
Tight job market	2.0	22	0.6	2
Other	14.4	159	17.0	61
TOTAL	100.1*	1106	99.9*	359

$x^2 = 49.6$; p = .00 with 7 d.f.

*Does not equal 100% due to rounding

Women were twice as likely as men to indicate location as a
primary consideration for accepting their most recent job.
Women were also more likely to cite the tight job market. In
contrast, a much higher proportion of men than women indicated
that status of the job or salary were most significant.

It is also apparent from an analysis of current job benefits
that women in the library profession have less access to financial support and leaves that may be important to career
advancement. Individuals in the COSWL study were asked to
indicate the amount of financial support they receive for
professional, continuing education, and research activities.
They were also asked to identify the extent to which they
receive released time from work for each activity. In every
category, a higher percentage of women than men received
neither financial nor released time support. In every
category a higher percentage of men than women received more
than 75% support of the costs of their professional
activities. No financial support for professional activities
was received by 32.9% (n=363) of the women, but only 21.4%
(n=75) of the men received no financial support. In contrast,
25.8% (n=282) of the women report receiving 75% or more of the
requested financial support compared to 33% (n=116) of the
men. Release time for professional activities was not given
to 14.4% (n=155) of the women and 9.2% (n=32) of the men.
Release time of 75% or more was given to only 36.5% (n=392) of
the women, but to 46.4% (n=162) of the men. Similar
differences were found throughout each of the categories
examined.

The data from the COSWL study do not reveal all the possible
causes for such differences in treatment between men and women
in the organization. Certainly the greater administrative
achievements of men may be related to their increased access

to financial and release time support. It is also possible
that women do not seek these benefits at the same rate, or do
not negotiate for them when taking a new job. Whatever the
sources of these differences, it is apparent from these data
that women members of ALA as a group do not have the administrative status of male members, nor do they have equal access
to those professional organizational resources that are important to advancement in the profession.

Professional Involvement

   Professional involvement at both the national and state
level was considered in the COSWL study. These findings are
summarized in table 10.
   The level of involvement of both women and men in ALA is
perhaps the most striking pattern that emerges, although it
should be remembered that since the COSWL study is one of an
association membership that these data probably do not represent professional involvement of librarians in general.
   The second fact that emerges is, once again, the disparity
between men and women in the association in terms of their
levels of achievement. At the national level, proportionally
twice as many men as women have been elected or appointed to
office or chaired a committee. Election or appointment to a
national position has been achieved by 14.7% (n=174) of the
women and 31.7% (n=120) of the men. Only 12.2% (n=145) of the
women report chairing a national committee as opposed to 28.2%
(n=107) of the men. At the state level, there are also significant differences in participation, with 38.8% (n=461) of
the women and 55.1% (n=209) of the men indicating they have
been elected or appointed to state or regional positions.
Chair of a committee has been held by 32.2% (n=382) of the
women compared to 49.9% (n=189) of the men.
   Publication, another important measure of professional involvement of librarians, is also more actively pursued by
men. Individuals were asked to indicate the extent to which
they have engaged in publishing, research, and presentation of
papers at conferences. In all categories, men are twice as
prolific as women. Among the more important findings are that
5.2% (n=62) of the women have written a book, compared to
17.1% (n=65) of the men. Papers at conferences have been presented by 14.9% (n=179) of the women and 33.7% (n=128) of the
men. More than half (52.5%, n=200) of the men have written
journal articles. Only 24.9% (n=298) of the women report such
publications. Finally, book reviews have been written by
18.8% (n=225) of the women and 35.7% (n=136) of the men. Similar findings have been reported in analyses of library publishing.

Table 10.   Professional Involvement at Different Levels by Sex

	Female		Male	
	%	N	%	N
Elected/appointed national position				
No	85.3	1012	68.3	259
Yes	14.7	174	31.7	120
$x^2 = 53.2$; p = .00 with 1 d.f.				
Chair, national committee				
No	87.8	1047	71.8	272
Yes	12.2	145	28.2	107
$x^2 = 54.0$; p = .00 with 1 d.f.				
Member, national committee				
No	56.9	674	36.8	139
Yes	43.1	510	63.2	239
$x^2 = 45.8$; p = .00 with 1 d.f.				
Elected/appointed state or regional position				
No	61.2	727	44.9	170
Yes	38.8	461	55.1	209
$x^2 = 30.7$; p = .00 with 1 d.f.				
Chair, state or regional committee				
No	67.8	803	50.1	190
Yes	32.2	382	49.9	189
$x^2 = 37.8$; p = .00 with 1 d.f.				
Member, state or regional committee				
No	39.3	469	28.1	107
Yes	60.7	724	71.9	274
$x^2 = 15.2$; p < .1 with 1 d.f.				

Salary Differences

After examination of these findings as a whole, it is apparent that there are significant differences in status between women and men in the library profession in the following areas: personal/familial, professional preparation, career pattern, and current employment. Any one of these differences might be expected to contribute to differences in status within the profession. The cross-sectional nature of the study and its restriction to members of one professional association limit the types of causal inferences that might be made about the way in which these aspects affect one another. Moreover,

there are significant, but different types of library jobs.
For example, the department head of a large academic library
is considered by many to have a higher-status job than an individual who is director of a small public library. One analysis that did seem to have potential for trying to understand
the effects of sex, background, and career variables on professional achievement was a multivariate analysis of the
answers to key questions using salary as the dependent variable. Within different types of libraries, however, there may
be different priorities placed on academic credentials, publishing, professional involvement, or other individual
achievements. Therefore salary patterns were examined by type
of library, rather than by combining all members of the sample
into one unit.

  As indicated above there are significant differences between
men and women in the association with regard to salaries
earned. These differences exist in all types of libraries
(table 11). Because of the small number of men employed in
school libraries, the regression analysis was appropriate for
only academic and public librarians in the study.

Table 11. Mean Salaries of Male and Female ALA Members by
           Type of Library Employment

	Academic	Public	School
Female	$14,850	$14,236	$14,725
Male	20,520	19,319	18,692

  Within these two types of libraries the following were examined: the effect on salary of age, sex, perceived mobility,
length of time since receiving the MLS degree, total time
spent on leave, number of books published, number of articles
published, organization size, number of professionals and nonprofessionals supervised, and number of levels in the organizational hierarchy above the individual. In this analysis,
simple correlations between any two of the variables were
examined first. Second, standard multivariate analysis was
applied to ascertain the extent to which each of the identified areas contributed to overall variation in salary in each
of the three types of libraries.

  There were wide variations in the relationships between salary and other variables in different types of libraries. Only
a few areas besides age, sex and date of receiving the MLS degree were strongly correlated (7.50) with salary. In academic
libraries, the number of professionals supervised ($r=.550$) and
the number of books published ($r=.328$) correlated with earnings.[1]

In public libraries, supervision of nonprofessionals
(r=.376) was related to salary; publication was not.

The complexity of these interrelationships and, in particular, the association of sex with rates of publication, supervisory responsibility, and even date of receiving the MLS
suggest the importance of allowing for the effects of personal
and professional variables on salary when examining differences in salary of men and women (tables 12 and 13).

As expected, the regression analyses of academic and public
librarians (tables 12 and 13) indicate that a significant proportion of the variance in salaries can be explained by age
and date of receiving the MLS degree. Librarians who are
older (Beta=-.086, F=2.29 for academic librarians; Beta=-.258,
F=19.63 for public librarians) or who have held the professional degree longer (Beta=-.106, F=41.44, for academics;
Beta=.167, F= 14.14 in academic libraries; and Beta=-.380,
F=41.18 for public librarians) receive higher salaries.

For both academic and public librarians, having published a
book is an important factor in salary determination
(Beta=.167, F=14.14 in academic libraries; and Beta=.103,
F=5.93 for public libraries).

Table 12. Salary of Academic Librarians by Personal,
           Professional, and Organizational Differences

	b	beta	F
Date of birth	-.020	-.086	2.29
Mobility	.077	.016	0.13
Date of MLS	-.106	-.393	41.44
Total amount of leave time	-.012	-.108	7.45
Books published	.554	.167	14.14
Articles published	-.014	-.015	3.02
Full-time employees in organization	.000	.012	0.09
Professionals supervised (FTE)	.103	.350	73.78
Nonprofessionals supervised (FTE)	.001	.017	.20
Level in organizational hierarchy	-.215	-.107	7.40
Sex	-.640	-.134	11.13

R^2	0.605
Standard error	1.507
b constant	50.531
F	40.574
N	303

Some difference exists between public and academic librarians in the relationship between organizational factors and salary. In academic libraries, the greater the number of professionals supervised (Beta=.350, F=73.78) and the fewer levels of organizational hierarchy above the individual (Beta=-.107, F= 7.40), the higher the librarian's salary. The size of the organization as measured by number of full-time employees and the number of nonprofessionals supervised were not found to be significant contributers to salary differences in academic libraries.

For public librarians, size of organization was important, with individuals in larger organizations earning higher salaries (Beta=.169, F=13.03). Librarians who have fewer people above them in the organizational hierarchy also earn higher salaries (Beta=-.110, F=5.04). Supervisory responsibility of public librarians is not clearly related to salary, however. In the sample of ALA members who are public librarians, the number of nonprofessionals supervised is positively related to salary (Beta=.401, F=18.64) but number of professionals supervised is negatively associated with salary (Beta=-.253, F=7.87). Without further study it is difficult to interpret

Table 13.   Salary of Public Librarians by Personal,
            Professional, and Organizational Differences

	b	beta	F
Date of birth	-.047	-.258	19.63
Mobility	.950	.022	0.25
Date of MLS	-.082	-.380	41.18
Total amount of leave time	-.006	-.111	6.33
Books published	.507	.103	5.93
Articles published	.002	.008	.04
Full-time employees in organization	.001	.169	13.03
Professionals supervised (FTE)	-.020	-.253	7.87
Nonprofessionals supervised (FTE)	.024	.401	18.64
Level in organizational hierarchy	-.159	-.110	5.04
Sex	-.881	-.168	14.29

$$R^2 \quad .570$$

Standard error   1.478
b constant   102.215
F   30.769
N   267

these findings. It may be that public librarians who are have greater responsibility in larger organizations are part of a more hierarchical system and therefore direct supervision of professionals may be limited. For example, the director of a large public library may consider the only professional for whom he or she is directly responsible is the assistant or associate director.

Most important to the COSWL study are the findings on sex and salary in the regression analysis. When each of the other factors is held constant, sex is an important determinant of salary for both academic (Beta=-.134, F=11.13) and public (Beta=-.168, F=14.29) librarians. That is, being male is significantly associated with receiving a higher salary even when personal, professional, and organizational variables are comparable to those of females in the sample.

4. Conclusions and Suggestions for Further Research

As stated at the outset of this report, the "overall purpose of the COSWL study was to provide data for evaluating the status of women in librarianship." Our findings support and expand those of other studies that have identified significant differences between the treatment of men and women in the library profession. Moreover, evidence suggests that salary discrimination for women exists even when one allows for the personal, career, and professional variations that contribute to salary differences. In terms of career preparation, women have had fewer employment opportunities that might lead to effective placements and initiation into "the old boy network." They also are less likely to have taken an advanced degree. Women's personal lives appear to be more limiting also, with a greater proportion of women than men reporting limits to mobility and job leaves for pregnancy, childcare, or family moves.

An analysis of employment patterns shows that women tend to hold proportionally fewer administrative positions than men. There is also some segregation by type of library, with almost half the men employed in academic situations. Men are also more likely to have had different jobs in different organizations.

Professional activities are engaged in at a much higher rate by men in ALA. At both the national and state/regional level, men are more likely to be officeholders. Publishing and other research activities are more actively pursued by men in the association than by women. Opportunities for engaging in such work appear to be more available to men than to women.

Finally, the most tangible evidence of difference is that of salary. In part, the significant differences in women and men's salaries are a function of those patterns cited above but it was also found that sex is important even when those personal and professional differences are controlled.

Despite the strength of the relationships in these findings, it would be a mistake to use them as a basis for an indictment of sexism in the library profession. The COSWL study was a one-time, cross-sectional study of members of one professional association. Therefore, only tentative suggestions can be made about the causal relationships between personal, professional, sex, and salary variables. For example, do men obtain higher academic administrative positions because they publish more? Or do they publish more because they are in academic administrative positions that encourage and support such work? Are women channeled into school and public library work by their academic institution? Or is such channeling a function of general socialization of women (perhaps from birth)? Many such questions arise when one examines these COSWL data. Yet, by observing a different professional situation for women, one must consider what changes are possible and what a professional organization can do to achieve parity.

One central point of concern that can be dealt with immediately is the issue of professional involvement of ALA members. As has been stated, the study finds women less involved in both professional association work and in publishing and research. At the same time, they do not have access to the same financial and release-time support as men. These are problems that can be addressed by the associations and library organizations. It may necessitate adjustment of library rules in situations in which only upper-level managers are given professional support, but it is an adjustment that could well enhance both the quality and nature of professional involvement of women in librarianship. Such an adjustment is particularly important when it is remembered that, on the whole, women have fewer family resources (i.e., less total family income) on which they might draw for support of professional activities.

Within library education, it may be possible to examine work-study placements and graduate assistantships to equalize opportunities for men and women to become part of those networks that become important for recommendations and job placement.

Other factors such as family obligations, limited mobility, and reasons for accepting certain types of positions may be less easily influenced by the professional association. This limitation does not mean, however, that such issues should be buried. It is important for professional associations to identify their relationship to occupational achievement and to help women think through the nature and consequences of such commitments. Guidance and other support, as well as additional research, should also be a function of the professional association interested in the professional development of all of its members.

Further Research

The COSWL study is one of the most comprehensive studies on
women in librarianship that has yet been done in that it examines many of the factors that are considered to contribute to
differences in achievement between men and women. It is, however limited, particularly, given the changing nature of librarianship today.

Future research on members of the library profession cannot
be limited to members of one association; affiliation with
ASIS, AIM, ALA, or SLA are just several options open to librarians. Moreover, a significant (and probably larger female) segment of the library population does not belong to any
association. It is necessary to know about those individuals
who are trained or who work as librarians in many types of organizations and also, in this economy, to know about those who
are no longer employed in the field.

Perhaps the most fruitful research that could be undertaken
at this point would be research that would follow-up cohort
groups from several different types of library schools. It
would enable researchers to look at tracking for library and
non-library work, at support and guidance systems, and even at
certain personality factors that might be important to professional differences. It would also provide data for causal
analysis of a number of the variables in the COSWL study.

The data from the COSWL study, while limited, also provide a
source that other researchers may wish to exploit. There is
no isolated analyses on retired ALA members, for example.
Those individuals who wish to work with these data are invited
to contact either of the principal investigators of the
study. At this time (June, 1982) there is a data tape at Syracuse University. At some future time, it is hoped that there
will be an additional tape at the University of Illinois and
in one of the existing data archives (e.g., the Schlesinger
Library). Individuals are also invited to contact either of
the investigators if there are questions about the data presented here.

One final note: a complementary objective of the investigators of this study was "to design a study that would contribute to the positive image of women in librarianship by
virtue of the quality of the research. Attention to methodology was seen to be important to assure that the study's findings would be taken seriously since criticism of methodology
is one of the easiest ways to dismiss research findings that
are unpalatable." In keeping with this objective, two
articles based on data from the study have been published. To
date, one, "A Profile of the ALA Membership," has been
included in Library Literature: The Best of 1981. The
concern over methodology and the limited funds that were
available for this study have made the investigators cautious,
however, in interpreting these data. Though the investigators
are comfortable with the conclusions presented here, other researchers might build creatively on this work.

Notes

Preface

1. Individuals interested in these data may contact the ALA Office for Library Personnel Resources, 50 E. Huron, Chicago, IL 60611, for further information.

Review of the Literature

1. Letter from Dolly Pither, Secretary to the Executive Director, Canadian Library Association to Kathleen M. Heim, September 24, 1979.

2. For an evaluation of this study see Futas, 1983.

3. The exceptions, of course, are research dissertations which often use library directories to establish a sample. These tend to focus on an aspect of librarians' careers rather than an overview. They are, therefore, discussed in connection with discrete variable formulation rather than the overview of demographics.

4. For a comprehensive discussion of the studies discussed in the Review of the Literature section see Heim (1982) which displays tabular economic data.

Analysis of Major Findings

1. The correlation coefficient ("r") measures the extent to which two variables occur together and ranges from "0" to "1" with "1" representing the situation in which two variables are always associated with one another. Variance (or "R^2") measures the extent to which the change in one (or a group) of variables is associated with a change in another.

Appendix: Questionnaire

AMERICAN LIBRARY ASSOCIATION

50 EAST HURON STREET · CHICAGO, ILLINOIS 60611 · (312) 944-6780

February 20, 1980

Dear American Library Association Member:

The enclosed questionnaire is being sent to you as part of
a national study of the career development of members of the
American Library Association. The research is being supported
by an award to the Association for that purpose and questionnaires
are being sent to a random sample of the membership.

The questions relate to your individual career patterns and
also ask about family and educational background. The latter
group has been included because previous studies of career
development of other professional groups have found these factors
to be important.

All responses will be strictly confidential. Neither the
questionnaires nor the return envelopes have been coded and
the identity of the respondent will not be known. We have
enclosed a self-addressed stamped post card and ask that you
return this at the time you mail the questionnaire. This
will enable us to determine who has returned the questionnaire
and will prevent our sending follow-up letters to those who have
already responded.

The questionnaire should take approximately 20 minutes to
complete. We ask that you return it by March 15, 1980. A
self-addressed, stamped envelope has been included for your
convenience.

Thank you very much for your support. If you have any
questions about the design of the study or its findings, we
would be happy to answer them for you.

Sincerely yours,

Thomas J. Galvin
President

Kathleen Heim
Assistant Professor
University of Illinois
Urbana-Champaign
Co-Principal

Leigh Estabrook
Associate Professor
Syracuse University
Co-Principal Investigator

1.   Please provide a brief summary of your career history since receiving the
        baccalaureate degree (if no B.A. held, begin with your first full time
        position). If you have held different positions within the same organ-
        ization, these should be listed separately. To preserve anonimity, you
        are asked only to indicate the _type_ (e.g. special library, state library
        agency, large business), not the name of the organization in which you
        worked. N.B. Please include all position, not just those in the
        library/information service profession.

Type of Organization	Job Title	Year Began	Year Left	Full Time	Part Time

A.____

B.____

C.____

D.____

E.____

F.____

G.____

H.____

I.____

(If additional space is needed, please attach separate sheet)

2.   Which one of these categories would best describe your general career pattern?

        _____I have held the same position within the same organization

        _____I have held similal positions within the same organization

        _____I have held different types of positions within the same organization

        _____I have held similar positions within different organizations

        _____I have held different types of positions within different organizations

3.   From the time you accepted your first professional position in the
     library/information service profession did you ever leave the field
     for a period of six months or more?

     ______No (Please skip to question 4)

     ______Yes

        If yes, please indicate the reasons why. For every reason that
        applies to you, please check a)the total number of leaves taken
        for this reason; and b)the total amount of time spent on leaves
        for this reason.

Reason for absence	Number of leaves taken	Total time spent on leave for this reason
To continue my education		
To work in another field		
Position was elimated		
Personal health reasons		
Health of family member		
I voluntarily resigned		
Pregnancy or child care		
Moved with spouse or friend		
Marriage or family reasons		
Military service		
I was terminated		
Other		

Section II: CURRENT OR MOST RECENT JOB SITUATION

*THE FOLLOWING SERIES OF QUESTIONS REFER TO THAT POSITION YOU
CURRENTLY HOLD, OR (IF YOU ARE NOT CURRENTLY EMPLOYED)
TO THAT MOST RECENTLY HELD*

4.   What would you say was your highest priority in your decision to accept
     your most recently held job?

     ______The status of the position

     ______The salary offered

     ______The challenge of the work required of the position

     ______The geographical location of the organization

     ______The opportunities for advancement offered by the position

     ______Other (Please specify)____

5.   At the time you began in this position, how would you have compared your professional qualifications and expertise to the requirements of the job?

       ______I felt underqualified for the position

       ______I was well suited to the position

       ______I felt overqualified for the position

6.   How long have you worked/did you work in that organization? _______Years.

7.   How is/was your job classified?   _______Part time   _______Full time

8.   Approximately how many full time employees are/were members of that organization (including both professional and non-professional)?

      about_______People

9.   How may individuals (full time equivalent) do/did you supervise?

     _______non-professionals   _______professionals

10.   In the organizational hierarchy, how many levels are/were above you? (The chief administrative officer counts as the highest level) _______________

11.   How much financial support has your organization been willing to give for professional activities?

	none	up to 25%	25 to 50%	50 to 75%	75% or more
Involvement with professional associations	___	___	___	___	___
Continuing education	___	___	___	___	___
Research	___	___	___	___	___

12.   How much released time has your organization been willing to give for professional activities?

	none	up to 25%	25 to 50%	50 to 75%	75% or more
Involvement with professional associations	___	___	___	___	___
Continuing education	___	___	___	___	___
Research	___	___	___	___	___

13.   Please summarize your formal educational background noting major field, dates you attended, and degrees received.

Degree	Major Field	Dates Attended	Date of Degree
Baccalaureate			
Masters (Please list all)			
Doctorate			

NOTE: IF NO BA OR EQUIVALENT RECEIVED, PLEASE GO TO QUESTION 18.

14.   From what type of undergraduate institution did you graduate? (for purposes of this study, a small college is one with a student body of less than 1200)

_____A small coeducational college/university

_____A large coeducational college/university

_____A small single sex college/university

_____A large single sex college/university

NOTE: If you have not pursued any formal education in library/information science, please skip to question 18.

15.   Did you work for money or tuition benefits while you studied for your first library/information science degree?

_____No

_____Yes

_____I worked within the school I was attending

_____I worked outside the school, in the library field

_____I worked outside the school, in another field

16.   During your work for the first degree in library/information science, did you receive any scholarships, fellowships, assistantships, or other awards?

_____No   _____Yes

17. What was your highest priority in your selection of a professional school?

      _______Its geographical location

      _______The reputation of the school

      _______The type of program offered by the school

      _______The reputation of certain faculty members of the school

      _______Other (Please specify)____

18. Have you ever been elected or appointed to a position at the national level in a professional association? _______No _______Yes

19. Have you ever been chair of a committee, section or division of a national professional association? _______No _______Yes

20. Have you ever been a member of a committee, section, or division of a national professional association? _______No _______Yes

21. Have you ever been elected or appointed to a position in a state or regional professional association? _______No _______Yes

22. Have you ever been chair of a committee, section, or division of a regional or state professional association? _______No _______Yes

23. Have you ever been a member of a committee, section or division of a state or regional professional association? _______No _______Yes

24. Please indicate the extent to which you have been involved in research and publishing.

Type of activity	Approximate number produced
Author of Book	
Editor or compiler of book or journal	
Journal or periodical article, author	
Technical paper	
Presented paper at state or national conference	
Published paper in state or national conference proceedings	
Research completed but manuscript unpublished	
Book reviews	

Section IV: PERSONAL AND FAMILY DATA

*THE FINAL SET OF QUESTIONS RELATE TO PERSONAL AND FAMILY DATA. AS INDICATED
IN THE COVER LETTER, NO INDIVIDUAL DATA WILL BE REPORTED NOR WILL THE INDI-
VIDUAL IDENTITY OF THE RESPONDENTS BE KNOWN BY ANYONE INCLUDING MEMBERS OF
THE RESEARCH TEAM.*

25.   In what year were you born? ________

26.   What is your sex? ______Female   ______Male

27.   What is your family status?

     ______Married

     ______Part of committed long-term relationship

     ______Divorced, separated or widowed

     ______Single

28.   Do you have any personal or familial responsibilities that limit your
mobility in job seeking? ______No   ______Yes

29.   What is your race?

     ______American Indian/Alaskan Native   ______White

     ______Asian American/American Oriental   ______Black

     ______Puerto Rican   ______Mexican American Chicano

     ______Other Spanish Surname

30.   What was your base salary, before taxes for the calendar year 1979? (Please
exclude extra compensation you may have received from consulting, summer school
or other sources. These are covered in the next question)

     ______Less than $9,000   ______$24,000 to $26,999

     ______$9,000 to $11,999   ______$27,000 to $29,999

     ______$12,000 to $14,999   ______$30,000 to $32,999

     ______$15,000 to $17,999   ______$33,000 to $35,999

     ______$18,000 t0 $20,999   ______$36,000 to $38,999

     ______$21,000 to $23,999   ______$39,000 to $41,999

                                                 ______$42,000 or Above

31.   What was your total family income before taxes for the calendar year 1979?

     ____ Less than $9,000   ______$24,000 to $26,999

     ______$9,000 to $11,999   ______$27,000 to $29,999

     ______$12,000 to $14,999   ______$30,000 to $32,999

     ______$15,000 to $17,999   ______$33,000 to $35,999

     ______$18,000 to $20,999   ______$36,000 to $38,999

     ______$21,000 to $23,999   ______$39,000 to $41,999

                                               ______$42,000 or Above

32. Are you now or have you ever been a parent or had legal custody of any children?
   _______No   _______Yes If yes, what are their present ages?_________________

33. Are you now or have you ever been responsible for any other dependents?
   _______No   _______Yes If yes, during what years? ____________________________

34. Are you presently seeking employment as a library/information professional?
   _______No   _______Yes If yes, what are your reasons? ___________________________
   ____

35. Could you please indicate the education and occupation of your parents while
   you were growing up and your spouse if you are married. If you are not
   married, please check "Not Applicable" in the appropriate box.

	Father	Mother	Spouse
Higest level of education			
Did not graduate from High School			
Graduated from High School			
Attended College-No degree			
Degree from four year college			
Some work on graduate level			
Graduate degree			
Not Applicable			
Occupation (Please Specify)			
Not Applicable			

36. How many children of each sex (including yourself) were in the family in
   which you were raised?

   _______Boys   _______Girls

37. How many children of each sex were younger than you?

   _______Boys were younger   _______Girls were younger

*THANK YOU VERY MUCH FOR YOUR TIME. PLEASE REMEMBER TO MAIL THE POSTCARD AT
THE SAME TIME THAT YOU RETURN THE QUESTIONNAIRE. WE WELCOME ADDITIONAL COM-
MENTS AND REQUESTS FOR COPIES OF THE RESEARCH FINDINGS.*

COMMENTS:

Bibliography

Materials on the status of women in librarianship which have
appeared since the present review of the literature was begun
will appear in the COSWL bibliography supplement, 1977 to
1981, to The Role of Women in Librarianship 1876-1976 (Weibel
and Heim, 1979).

"AIM Profiles the Information Management Professional." The
  Information Manager 2 (Spring 1980): 32-33.
AMEG Commission on Sex Bias in Measurement. "A Case History
  of Change: A Review of Responses to the Challenge of Sex
  Bias in Career Interest Inventories." Measurement and Eval-
  uation in Guidance 10 (October 1977): 148-52.
Ad Hoc Committee on the Status of Women in the Archival
  Profession. Report on the Status of Women in the Archival
  Profession. Philadelphia, Pa.: Society of American Archi-
  vists, August 29, 1974.
Almquist, Elizabeth McTaggart. Minorities, Gender and Work.
  Lexington, Mass.: D. C. Heath, 1979.
  ______. "Minority Men and Women at Work" in Minorities,
  Gender, and Work. Lexington, Mass.: Lexington Books, 1979.
  ______, and Angrist, S. S. "Career Salience and Atypicality
  of Occupational Choice among College Women." Journal of
  Marriage and the Family 32 (1970): 242-49.
Altman, S.L. "Women's Career Plans and Maternal Employment."
  Psychology of Women Quarterly 1 (4) (Summer 1977): 365-76.
Altus, William B. "Birth Order and Its Sequelae." Science
  151 (January 7, 1966): 44-48.
Alvarez, R. S. "Qualifications of Heads of Libraries in
  Cities of over 10,000 Population in the Seven North-Central
  States." Ph.D. dissertation, University of Chicago, 1939.

American Library Association, Association of Specialized and
    Cooperative Library Agencies. Salary Data-State Library
    Agencies. Chicago: ALA/ASCLA, December 1980.
American Library Association, Office for Library Personnel
    Resources. Degrees and Certificates Awarded by U.S. Library
    Education Programs 1973-1976. Chicago: ALA/OLPR, n.d.
    (Mimeographed.)
    ______. Degrees and Certificates Awarded by U.S. Library
    Education Programs 1976-1979. Chicago: ALA/OLPR, August
    1980. (Mimeographed.)
    ______. The Racial, Ethnic and Sexual Composition of Library
    Staff in Academic and Public Libraries. Chicago: ALA/OLPR,
    1981.
Anderson, R. "Motive to Avoid Success." Sex Roles 4 (April
    1978): 239-48.
Angrist, S. S. "Changes in Women's Work Aspirations during
    College or Work Does Not Equal Career." International Jour-
    nal of Sociology of the Family 2 (March 1972): 87-97.
    ______. "Measuring Women's Career Commitment." Sociological
    Focus 5 (Winter 1972): 29-39.
Anshen, R. The Family: Its Function and Destiny. New York:
    Harper, 1949.
Astin, Helen S. "Factors Affecting Women's Scholarly
    Productivity." In The Higher Education of Women: Essays in
    Honor of Rosemary Park. Helen S. Astin and Werner Hirsch,
    eds. New York: Praeger, 1978.
    ______. The Woman Doctorate in America: Origins, Career, and
    Family. New York: Russell Sage Foundation, 1969.
    ______. and Bayer, Alan E. "Sex Discrimination in Academe."
    The Educational Record 53 (Spring 1972): 101-18.
Avery, Clift. "An Analysis of Selected Factors in Relation to
    the Program Choices of Adult Undergraduate Women in Continu-
    ing Education." Ph.D. dissertation, Connecticut University,
    1977.
Badke, Bruce Edward. "The Relationship between the Person-
    ality Needs, Vocational Interests, and Career Orientation of
    College Women Using the Tern Activities Index, Holland's
    Typology, and the Vocational Preference Inventory." Ph.D.
    dissertation, Ohio State University, 1977.
Bardwick, J. M., ed. Readings on the Psychology of Women.
    New York: Harper & Row, 1972. (See E. D. Maccoby, "Sex
    Differences in Intellectual Functioning," pp.34-48.)
Barron, Paula Suzzanne England. "A Comparison of the
    Individual Characteristics, Extrinsic Rewards and Occupa-
    tional Mobility of Women in Male and Female Occupations."
    Ph.D. dissertation, University of Chicago, 1975.
Bartlett, Beatrice and Baines, Elizabeth. "Women's Vitae and
    the Problem of Perceiving Competence." Request from Ameri-
    can Educational Research Association, 1230 17th St. NW,
    Washington, D. C. 20036.

Baxter, S. G. "Analysis of Membership in the American Library Association Held by Individuals and Institutions in Texas in 1957." Texas Library Journal 35 (December 1959): 118-21.

Bayer, Alan E. "Birth Order and Attainment of the Doctorate: A Test of Economic Hypotheses." The American Journal of Sociology 72 (1967): 540-50.

Beach, B. H. "Expert Judgment about Uncertainty: Bayesian Decision Making in Realistic Settings." Organizational Behavior and Human Performance 14 (August 1975): 10-59.

Becker, G. S. Economics of Discrimination. Chicago: University of Chicago Pr., 1971.

__________. Human Capital. New York: National Bureau of Economic Research, 1975.

Becker, Howard S., and Campbell, James W. "The Development of Identification with an Occupation." American Journal of Sociology 61 (January 1956): 289-98.

Beckman, Linda J. "The Relative Rewards and Costs of Parenthood and Employment for Employed Women." Psychology of Women Quarterly 2 (Spring 1978): 215-34.

Bedeian, Arthur. "The Roles of Self-Esteem and Achievement in Aspiring to Prestigious Vocations." Journal of Vocational Behavior 11 (August 1977): 109-19.

Bergmann, Barbara R. "The Effect on White Incomes of Discrimination in Employment." Journal of Political Economy 79 (March/April 1971): 294-313.

Bernard, Jessie S. Academic Women. University Park: Pennsylvania State University Pr., 1964.

__________. "Historical and Structural Barriers to Occupational Desegregation." Signs 1 (Spring 1976): 87-94.

__________. Women and the Public Interest. Chicago: Aldine, 1971.

Besyner, J. K.; Bodden, J. L.; and Winer, J. L. "Differentiation of Holland's Personality Types of Means of Psychological Need Variables." Measurement and Evaluation in Guidance 10 (1977): 237-40.

Betz, Ellen L. "Vocational Behavior and Career Development, 1976: A Review." Journal of Vocational Behavior 11 (October 1977): 129-52.

Bidlack, Russell E. "Faculty." In 1980 Association of American Library Schools: Library Education Statistical Report, F1-F98. State College, Pa.: Association of American Library Schools, October 1980.

__________. "Faculty Availability in Terms of Affirmative Action." Ann Arbor: University of Michigan School of Library Science, March 14, 1979. (Mimeographed.)

__________. "Faculty Salaries of 62 Library Schools, 1975-76." Journal of Education for Librarianship 16 (Spring 1976): 258-70.

__________. "Faculty Salaries of 62 Library Schools, 1976-77." Journal of Education for Librarianship 17 (Spring 1977): 199-213.

__________. "Faculty Salaries of 62 Library Schools, 1977-78."
Journal of Education for Librarianship 18 (Spring 1978):
251-67.

__________. "A Statistical Survey of 67 Library Schools, 1978-79."
Journal of Education for Librarianship 19 (Spring 1979):
318-36.

Bielby, D. D. V. "Maternal Employment and Socioeconomic-
Status as Factors in Daughters Career Salience-Some
Substantive Refinements." Sex Roles 4 (April 1978):
249-65.

Blankenship, W. C. "Head Librarians: How Many Men? How Many
Women?" College and Research Libraries 28 (January 1967):
41-48.

Blau, Francine D. Equal Pay in the Office. Lexington, Mass.:
D. C. Heath, 1977.

__________. "Longitudinal Patterns of Female Labor Force Partici-
pation." In U. S. Department of Labor, Manpower Monograph, Dual Careers: A Longitudinal Study of the Labor
Market Experience of Women volume 4, pp. 27-55, ed. by
Herbert S. Parnes. Washington, D.C.: Govt. Printing Office,
1976.

__________, and Hendricks, Wallace E. "Occupational Segregation
by Sex: Trends and Prospects." Journal of Human Resources
14 (1979): 197-210.

Blau, Francine D., and Jusenius, Carol L. "Economists'
Approaches to Sex Segregation in the Labor Market: An Ap-
praisal." Signs 1 (Spring 1976): 181-200.

Blau, Peter M., and Duncan, Otis Dudley. The American Occupational Structure. New York: John Wiley, 1967.

Blaxall, Martha and Reagan, Barbara B., eds. "Women and the
Workplace: The Implications of Occupational Segregation."
Signs 1 (Spring 1976).

Bloomfield, Masse. "The Writing Habits of Librarians."
College and Research Libraries 27 (March 1966): 109-19.

Bob, Sharon. "The Myth of Equality: Financial Support for
Males and Females." Journal of College Student Personnel
18 (May 1977): 235-38.

Bose, Christine E. Jobs and Gender: Sex and Occupational
Prestige. Baltimore: Center for Metropolitan Planning and
Research, Johns Hopkins University, 1973.

Boulding, Elise. "Familiar Constraints of Women's Work Roles."
Signs 1 (Spring 1976): 95-117.

Boulding, Kenneth. "The Social Institutions of Occupational
Segregation Comment." Signs 1 (Spring 1976): 75-77.

Bradley, B. W. "A Study of Characteristics, Qualifications
and Succession Patterns of Heads of Large U.S. Academic and
Public Libraries." Master's thesis, University of Texas,
1968.

Braunagel, Judith Schiek. "Job Mobility as Related to Labor
Progression of Female Academic Librarians in the South."
Ph.D. dissertation, Florida State University, 1975.

______. "Job Mobility of Men and Women Librarians and How It Affects Career Advancement." American Libraries 10 (December 1979): 643-47.

Brief, Arthur P., and Wallace, Marc J. "The Impact of Employee Sex and Performance on the Allocation of Organizational Awards." Journal of Psychology 92 (January 1976): 25-34.

Brief, Arthur P.; Sell, Mary Van; and Aldag, Ramon J. "Vocational Decision Making among Women: Implications for Organizational Behavior." Academy of Management Review 4 (October 1979): 521-30.

Brown, George H. Degree Awards to Women: An Update. Washington, D. C.: National Center for Education Statistics, 1979.

Brugh, Anne E., and Beede, Benjamin R. "American Librarianship: Review Essay." Signs 1 (Summer 1976): 943-55.

Bryan, A. I. The Public Librarian: A Report of the Public Library Inquiry of the Social Science Research Council. New York: Columbia University Pr., 1952.

Buck, Vernon E. "Toward Professionals Managing Professionals: A Case Study of Career Development for Women Librarians." In The Evaluation of Continuing Education for Professionals: A Systems View, pp. 197-219, ed. by Preston L. LeBreton and Kathleen A. J. Murphy. Seattle: University of Washington, 1979.

Bundy, M. L., and Wasserman, P. The Academic Library Administrator and His Situation. Final Report. Bethesda, Md.: ERIC Document Reproduction Service, May 1970. ED 054 796.

______. The Administrator of a Special Library or Information Center and His Situation. Bethesda, Md.: ERIC Document Reproduction Service, 1972. ED 054 799.

______. The Public Library Administrator and His Situation. Urbana Information Series Publication No. 6. College Park, Md.: Urbana Information Interpreters, 1972.

Bundy, M. L. et al. The School Library Supervisor and Her Situation. Final Report. Bethesda, Md.: ERIC Document Reproduction Service, August 1970. ED 054 797.

Burke, Ronald J., and Weir, Tamara. "Some Personality Differences between Members of One Career and Two Career Families." Journal of Marriage and the Family 38 (August 1976): 453-59.

Burlin, F. "Focus of Control and Female Occupational Aspiration." Journal of Counseling Psychology 23 (March 1976): 126-29.

Burron, Martha G. Developing Women Managers: What Needs to Be Done? New York: Amacom, 1978.

Cameron, Donald F., and Heim, Peggy. The Economics of Librarianship in College and University Libraries, 1969-70. Washington, D.C.: Council on Library Resources, 1970.

______. How Well Are They Paid? Washington, D.C.: Council on Library Resources, 1972.

______. Librarians in Higher Education. Washington, D.C.:
   Council on Library Resources, 1974.
Cameron, Susan Wilson. "Women Faculty in Academia:
   Sponsorship, Informal Networks, and Scholarly Success."
   Ph.D. dissertation, University of Michigan, 1978.
Caplow, Theodore. The Sociology of Work. Minneapolis:
   University of Minnesota Pr., 1954.
______, and McGee, Reece J. The Academic Marketplace. New
   York: Basic Books, 1958.
Carnegie Commission on Higher Education. Opportunities for
   Women in Higher Education. New York: McGraw-Hill, 1973.
Carpenter, E. S. "Women in Male Dominated Health Profes-
   sions." International Journal of Health Services 7
   (1977): 191-202.
Carpenter, R. L., and Shearer, K. D. "Public Library Support
   and Salaries in the Seventies." Library Journal 101
   (March 15, 1976): 777-83.
______. "Sex and Salary Survey: Selected Statistics of Large
   Public Libraries in U.S. and Canada." Library Journal 97
   (November 15, 1972): 3682-85.
______. "Sex and Salary Update." Library Journal 99
   (January 15, 1974): 101-7.
Catalyst. Two-Career Families: A Bibliography of Relevant
   Readings. New York: Catalyst, 1980.
Centra, John. Women, Men and the Doctorate. Princeton, N.J.:
   Educational Testing Service, 1974.
Chafe, William Henry. The American Woman: Her Changing
   Social, Economic and Political Roles, 1920-1970. New York:
   Oxford University Pr., 1972.
Chase, Fran. "A Comparison of Men's and Women's Intergen-
   erational Mobility in the United States." American
   Sociological Review 40 (August 1975): 483-505.
Cheda, Sherrill; Fischer, Linda; Wasylycia-Coe, Mary Ann; and
   Yaffe, Phyllis. "Salary Differentials of Female and Male
   Librarians in Canada." Emergency Librarian 5 (January,
   February 1978): 3-13.
Clayton, H. An Investigation into Personality Characteristics
   among Library School Students at One Midwestern University.
   Bethesda, Md.: ERIC Document Reproduction Service, July
   1968. ED 024 422.
Clift, Robert Benjamin. "The Personality and Occupational
   Stereotype of Public Librarians." Ph.D. dissertation, Uni-
   versity of Minnesota, 1976.
Cohen, Eva D. Women in Medicine-A Survey of Professional
   Activities, Career Interpretations and Conflict Resolu-
   tions. New Haven, Conn.: Yale University Office of Region-
   al Activities and Continuing Education, 1975.
Cohn, William Loewy. "Factors in the Career Decisions and
   Position Choices by the Directors of Libraries at the
   State-Supported-Senior Colleges of Florida." Ph.D. disser-
   tation, Florida State University, 1972.

Collins, Randall. "A Conflict Theory of Sexual Stratifi-
cation." Social Problems 19 (Summer 1971): 3-21.
Cooper, Michael D. California's Demand for Librarians:
Projecting Future Requirements. Berkeley: University of
California, Institute for Governmental Studies, 1978.
______. "What the Numbers Say: A Statistical Portrait of
Librarians." American Libraries 7 (June 1976): 327-30.
Corcoran, Mary, and Duncan, Greg J. "Work History, Labor
Force Attachment and Earnings Differences between the Races
and Sexes." Journal of Human Resources 14 (Winter 1979):
3-20.
Corwin, M. A. "Investigation of Female Leadership in
Regional, State and Local Library Associations, 1876-1923."
Library Quarterly 44 (April 1974): 133-44.
Coser, Rose, and Rakoff, Gerald. "Women in the Occupational
World: Social Disruptions and Conflict." Social Problems
18 (1971): 535-54.
Covel, Janice Irene Mason. "Analysis of School Administrators'
Careers in Riverside County from 1870-71--1974-75: A Study
of Factors Which Affect Career Patterns for Men and Women in
School Organizations." Ph.D. dissertation, University of
California, Riverside, 1977.
Crawford, Jim D. "Career Development and Career Choice in
Pioneer and Traditional Women." Journal of Vocational Be-
havior 12 (April 1978): 129-39.
Cristo, Mary Gallagher. "Factors Influencing Career Mobility
and Career Attainment of Women in the Field of Education."
Ph.D. dissertation, University of Virginia, 1975.
Curby, Vicki Morgan. "Geographic Mobility of Women Adminis-
trators in Higher Education." Ph.D. dissertation,
University of Missouri, Columbia, 1978.
Dale, Doris C. "Career Patterns of Women Librarians with
Doctorates." University of Illinois Graduate School of Li-
brary Science Occasional Papers no. 147, December 1980.
Daniels, Arlene Kaplan. "Consequences of the Women's Move-
ment." A Survey of Research Concerns on Women's Issues.
Washington, D.C.: Association of American Colleges 1975:
5-7.
Denis, Laurent-Germain. "Academic and Public Librarians in
Canada: A Study of the Factors Which Influence Graduates of
Canadian Library Schools in Making Their First Career De-
cision in Favor of Academic or Public Libraries." Ph.D.
dissertation, Rutgers University, 1970.
Deutrich, Mabel E. "Ms. versus Mr. Archivist: An Update."
SAA Women's Caucus Newsletter 5 (March 1981): 3-6.
______. "Women in Archives: Ms. versus Mr. Archivist."
American Archivist 36 (April 1973): 171-81.
______. "Women in Archives: A Summary Report of the
Committee on the Status of Women in the Archival Profes-
sion." American Archivist 38 (January 1975): 43-46.

Deutrich, Mabel E., and DeWhitt, Ben. "The Society of
   American Archivists." The American Archivist 43 (Fall
   1980): 527-35.
   ______, and Campbell, Ann Morgan, eds. "Survey of the Archival
   Profession-1979." American Archivist 43 (Fall 1980):
   527-35.
DeWath, Nancy V., and Cooper, Michael D. 1981-82 Library Human
   Resources: A Study of Supply and Demand. Rockville, Md.:
   King Research, December 1980. (Mimeographed).
Diamond, Esther E., ed. Issues of Sex Bias and Sex Fairness
   in Career Interest Measurement. Washington, D.C.: Depart-
   ment of Health, Education and Welfare, National Institute of
   Education, Career Education Program, 1975.
Dinerman, Beatrice. "Sex Discrimination in Academia."
   Journal of Higher Education 42 (1971): 253-64.
Dipboye, Robert L., and Wiley, Jack W. "Reactions of College
   Recruiters to Interviewer Sex and Self-Presentation Style."
   Journal of Vocational Behavior 10 (February 1977): 1-12.
Douglas, Priscilla Delahunt. "An Analysis of Demographic
   Characteristics and Career Patterns of Women Administrators
   in Higher Education." Ph.D. dissertation, University of
   Connecticut, 1976.
Douglass, R. R. "Personality of the Librarian." Ph.D.
   dissertation, University of Chicago, 1957.
Drennen, H. T., and Darling, R. L. "The Public Librarian."
   In Library Manpower: Occupational Characteristics of Public
   and School Librarians, pp. 1-14. Washington, D.C.: Govt.
   Printing Office, 1966.
Dudley, G. A., and Tideman, D. V. Career Development.
   Muncie, In.: Accelerated Development, 1977.
Duncan, O. D.; Featherman, David L.; and Duncan, Beverly.
   Socioeconomic Background and Achievement. New York: Semi-
   nar Pr., 1972.
Duncan, R. P., and Perrucci, C. C. "Dual Occupation Families
   and Migration." American Sociological Review 41 (April
   1976): 252-61.
Dworak, Marcia. "Women in Public Library Management: How Do
   They Measure Up?" Public Library Quarterly 1 (Summer
   1979): 147-60.
Dynes, Russell; Clarke, Alfred C.; and Dinetz, Simon. "Levels
   of Occupational Aspiration: Some Aspects of Family Exper-
   ience on a Variable." American Sociological Review 21
   (April 1956): 212-15.
Edsall, Shirley Ann. "Career Patterns of Community College
   Librarians." Ph.D. dissertation, Indiana University,
   Bloomington, 1973.
Educational Research Services, Inc. National Survey of Sal-
   aries and Wages in Public Schools, 1979-80. Arlington, Va.:
   ERS, 1980.

Eichler, Margrit. "Sociological Research on Women in Canada."
    The Canadian Review of Sociology and Anthropology 12
    (November, 1975): 474-81.
Ennis, Philip H., and Winger, Howard W. Seven Questions about
    the Profession of Librarianship. Chicago: University of
    Chicago, 1962.
Epstein, Cynthia F. "Encountering the Male Establishment:
    Sex-Status Limits on Women's Careers in the Professions."
    American Journal of Sociology 75 (May 1970): 965-82.
    ______. Woman's Place: Options and Limits in Professional
    Careers. Berkeley, Calif.: University of California Pr.,
    1970.
Epstein, Gilda F., and Bronzaft, Arline L. "Female Modesty in
    Aspiration Level." Journal of Counseling Psychology 21
    (January 1974): 57-60.
Equal Pay for Equal Work: Women in Special Libraries. New
    York: Special Libraries Association, 1976.
Estabrook, Leigh S., and Heim, Kathleen M. "A Profile of ALA
    Personal Members." American Libraries 11 (December 1980):
    654-59.
Estes, Mark E. "The Southern California Association of Law
    Libraries 1979 Salary Survey: Another Regional Reflection
    of a National Pattern?" Law Library Journal 72 (Summer
    1979): 526-33.
Etaugh, C. "Effects of Maternal Employment on Children:
    Review of Recent Research." Merrill-Palmer Quarterly of
    Behavior and Development 20 (April 1974): 71-98.
Etzioni, Amitai. The Semi-Professions and Their Organiza-
    tion. New York: Free Press, 1969.
Eyde, Lorraine Dittrich. Work Values and Background Factors
    as Predictors of Women's Desire to Work. Bureau of Business
    Research Monograph no. 108. Columbus: Ohio State Univer-
    sity, 1962.
Farley, R. A. "The American Library Executive: An Inquiry
    into His Concepts of the Function of His Office." Ph.D.
    dissertation, University of Illinois, 1967. (DAI Number:
    67-11851.)
Farmer, Helen S. "What Inhibits Achievement and Career Moti-
    vation in Women?" Counseling Psychologist 6 (1976): 12-15.
    ______. What Inhibits Achievement and Career Motivation in
    Women? Why Women Contribute Less to the Humanities, Arts,
    and Sciences. Bethesda, Md.: ERIC Document Reproduction
    Service, 1976. ED 130 943.
Featherman, David L. and Hanson, Robert M. "Sexual Inequal-
    ities and Socioeconomic Achievement in the U.S., 1962-1974."
    American Sociological Review 41 (June 1976): 462-83.
Fecher, Agnes Anne Rohlof. "Career Patterns of Women in
    College and University Administration." Ph.D. dissertation,
    Indiana University, 1972.

Feild, Hubert S., and Caldwell, Barbara E.   "Sex of Super-
     visor, Sex of Subordinate, and Subordinate Job Satisfaction."
     Psychology of Women Quarterly 3 (Summer 1979): 391-99.
Fennell, Janice Clinedinst.   "A Career Profile of Women Direc-
     tors of the Largest Academic Libraries in the United
     States: An Analysis and Description of Determinants."
     Ph.D. dissertation, Flordia State University, 1978.
Ferber, Marianne, and Huber, Joan.   "Husbands, Wives and
     Careers." Journal of Marriage and the Family 41 (May
     1979): 315-25.
Filter, Nancy H.   "Selected Characteristics of Members of the
     Music Library Association." Research paper at Kent State
     University Library School, May 11, 1969.
     ______, and Marco, Guy A.   "MLA: A Membership Profile." MLA
     Notes 26 (March 1970): 487-90.
Fischer, Linda; Wasylycia-Coe, Mary Ann; Cheda, Sherrill; and
     Yaffe, Phyllis. The Career Paths of Male and Female Librar-
     ians in Canada: Report to the Canada Council. Supported by
     Canada Council Grant. S74-1740.
Fisher, Francine Priscilla.   "A Study of the Relationship
     between the Security of Women in Educational Administrative
     Positions and the Multiple Factors Which Influence the
     Career Aspirations of Women Teachers." Ph.D. dissertation,
     Michigan State University, 1978.
Fottler, Myron D., and Bain, Trevor.   "Research Notes: Sex
     Differences in Occupational Aspirations." Academy of Manage-
     ment Journal 23 (March 1980): 144-49.
Frank, Robert H.   "Why Women Earn Less: The Theory and
     Estimation of Differential Overqualification." American
     Economic Review 68 (June 1978): 360-73.
Frankie, Suzanne. ARL Annual Salary Survey 1976-77.
     Washington, D.C.: Association of Research Libraries, 1977.
     ______. Association of Research Libraries Annual Salary
     Survey 1977-1978. Washington, D.C.: Association of Research
     Libraries, November, 1978.
Frarey, Carlyle J., moderator.   "Law Library Salaries." Law
     Library Journal 63 (November 1970): 471-504.
     ______, and Learmont, C. L.   "Placements and Salaries, 1972:
     We Held Our Own." Library Journal 98 (June 15, 1973):
     1880-86.
     ______. "Placement and Salaries, 1973: Not Much Change."
     Library Journal 99 (July 1974): 1767-74.
     ______. "Placement and Salaries, 1974: Promise or
     Illusion?" Library Journal 100 (October 1, 1975): 1767-74.
Freeman, Bonnie Cook.   "Faculty Women in the American
     University: Up the Down Staircase." Higher Education 6
     (May 1977): 165-88.
Fretwell, Gordon, comp. ARL Annual Salary Survey 1978-1979.
     Washington, D.C.: Association of Research Libraries, Febru-
     ary 1980.

______. Association of Research Libraries Annual Salary
Survey 1979-1980. Washington, D.C.: Association of Research
Libraries, December, 1980.

Furniss, W. Todd, and Graham, Patricia A., eds. Women in
Higher Education. Washington, D.C.: American Council on Education, 1974.

Futas, Elizabeth. "An Analysis of the Study, 'Career Paths of
Male and Female Librarians in Canada.'" In The Status of
Women in Librarianship: Historical, Sociological and Eco-
nomic Issues, pp. 393-423, ed. by Kathleen M. Heim. New
York: Neal-Schuman, 1983.

Gardner, Helen Rogers. "Women Administrators in Higher
Education in Illinois." Ph.D. dissertation, Indiana University, 1966.

Gasser, Mary Helen. "Career Patterns of Women Administrators
in Higher Education." Ph.D. dissertation, Southern Illinois
University at Carbondale, 1975.

Ghaffari-Samai, Parvine. "An Analysis of Selected Factors Related to Occupational Aspirations and Expectations of Adult
Women." Ph.D. dissertation, University of Connecticut, 1979.

Ginzberg, Eli. Good Jobs, Bad Jobs, No Jobs. Cambridge,
Mass.: Harvard University Pr., 1979.

______. Life Styles of Educated Women. New York: Columbia
University Pr., 1966.

______. "Toward a Theory of Occupational Choice: A Restate-
ment." Vocational Guidance Quarterly 20 (March 1972):
169-76.

Ginzberg, Eli; Ginsburg, Sol W.; Axelrad, Sidney; and Herman,
John L. Occupational Choice: An Approach to a General
Theory. New York: Columbia University Pr., 1951.

Ginzberg, Eli, and Yahaler, Alice M. Educated American Women:
Self-Portraits. New York: Columbia University Pr., 1966.

Glenn, Norval; Ross, Andreain H.; and Tully, Judy Cordur.
"Patterns of Intergenerational Mobility of Females through
Marriage." American Sociological Review 39 (October
1974): 683-99.

Gold, Alice R. "Reexamining Barriers to Women's Career
Development." American Journal of Orthopsychiatry 48 (October 1978): 690-702.

Goldstein, Rachael K. "Women and Health Sciences Librarianship: An Overview." MLA Bulletin 65 (July 1977):
321-29.

Goldstein, Rachael K., and Hill, Dorothy R. "The Status of
Women in the Administration of Health Science Libraries."
Bulletin of the Medical Library Association 63 (October
1975): 386-95.

______. "The Status of Women in the Administration of Health
Sciences Libraries: A Five Year Follow-up Study, 1972-1977."
Bulletin of the Medical Library Association 68 (January
1980): 6-15.

Goodale, James C., and Hall, Douglas T. "Inheriting a Career: The Influence of Sex, Values, and Parents." *Journal of Vocational Behavior* 8 (February 1976): 19-30.

Gottfredson, G. D., and Holland, J. L. "Vocational Choices of Men and Women: A Comparison of Predictors from the Self-Directed Search." *Journal of Counseling Psychology* 22 (January 1975): 28-34.

Grandjean, B. D., and Bernal, H. H. "Sex and Centralization in a Senior-Profession." *Sociology of Work and Occupations* 6 (February 1979): 84-102.

Greenfield, Susan T. "Attitudes toward Work and Success of Women Employed in Male versus Female-Dominated Jobs." Ph.D. dissertation, University of Southern California, 1978.

Greenhau, Jeffrey H. "Career Salience as a Moderator of Relationship between Satisfaction with Occupational Preference and Satisfaction with Life in General." *Journal of Psychology* 86 (January 1974): 53-55.

______, and Simon, William E. "Career Salience, Work Values, and Vocational Indecision." *Journal of Vocational Behavior* 10 (February 1977): 104-10.

Griffiths, Martha W. "Can We Still Afford Occupational Segregation? Some Remarks." *Signs* 1 (Spring 1976): 7-14.

Grimm, James W., and Stern, Robert N. "Sex Roles and Internal Labor Market Structures: The 'Female' Semi-Professions." *Social Problems* 21 (June 1974): 690-705.

Gross, E. "Plus or Change. . . ? The Sexual Structure of Occupations over Time." *Social Problems* 16 (Fall 1968): 198-208.

Halaby, Charles N. "Sexual Inequality in the Workforce: An Employer Specific Analysis of Pay Differences." *Social Science Research* 8 (March 1979): 79-104.

Hall, Anna C. *An Analysis of Certain Professional Library Occupations in Relation to Formal Educational Objectives.* Pittsburgh: Carnegie Library, 1968.

Hall, Douglas T. "Pressures from Work, Self, and Home in the Life Stages of Married Women." *Journal of Vocational Behavior* 6 (February 1975): 121-32.

______, and Gordon, F. E. "Career Choices of Married Women: Effects on Conflict, Role Behavior, and Satisfaction." *Journal of Applied Psychology* 58 (August 1973): 42-48.

Hall, Richard. *Occupations and the Social Structure.* Englewood Cliffs, N.J.: Prentice-Hall, 1969.

Hamovitch, William, and Morgenstern, Richard D. "Children and the Productivity of Academic Women." *Journal of Higher Education* 48 (November/December 1977): 633-45.

Harneer, Martina S. "Toward an Understanding of Achievement Related Conflicts in Women." *Journal of Social Issues* 28 (1972): 157-75.

Hartman, Heid. "Capitalism, Patriarchy, and Job Segregation by Sex." *Signs* 1 (Spring 1976): 137-69.

Harvey, J. F. The Librarian's Career: A Study of Mobility.
ACRL Microcard Series no. 85. Rochester, N.Y.: University
of Rochester Pr. for the Association of College and Research
Libraries, 1957.

Hawley, P. "Perceptions of Male Models of Femininity Related
to Career Choice." Journal of Counseling Psychology 19
(July 1972): 318-22.

Heim, Kathleen M. "The Demographic and Economic Status of
Librarians in the Seventies, with Special Reference to
Women." In Advances in Librarianship volume 12, ed. by
Wesley Simonton. New York: Academic Pr., 1982.

Heim, Kathleen M., and Kacena, C. "Sex, Salaries, and Library
Support." Library Journal 104 (March 15, 1979): 675-80.

________. "Sex, Salaries and Library Support . . . 1979."
Library Journal 105 (January 1, 1980): 17-22.

Hennig, Margaret Marie. "Career Development for Women
Executives." Ph.D. dissertation, Harvard University, 1971.

Hiller, Dana V., and Philliber, William W. "The Derivation of
Status Benefits from Occupational Attainments of Working
Wives." Journal of Marriage and the Family 40 (February
1978): 63-69.

Hoffman, Lois W., and Nye, F. Ivan. Working Mothers: An
Evaluative Review of the Consequences for Wife, Husband, and
Child. San Francisco: Jossey-Bass, 1975.

Holcomb, William R., and Anderson, Wayne P. "Vocational
Guidance Research: A Five-Year Overview." Journal of Vocational Behavior 10 (August 1977): 341-46.

Holland, John L. Making Vocational Choices: A Theory of
Careers. Englewood Cliffs, N.J.: Prentice-Hall, 1973.

________. The Psychology of Vocational Choice. Waltham, Mass.:
Blaisdell, 1966.

________, and Holland, J. E. "Vocational Indecision: More
Evidence and Speculation." Journal of Counseling Psychology 24 (1977): 404-14.

Holmstrom, Lynda Lytle. "Intertwining Career Patterns of
Husbands and Wives in Certain Professions." Ph.D. dissertation, Brandeis University, 1970.

________. The Two Career Family. Cambridge, Mass.: Schenkman,
1972.

Howell, Frank M.; Frese, Wolfgang; and Sollie, Carlton R.
"Ginzberg's Theory of Occupational Choice: A Reanalysis of
Increasing Realism." Journal of Vocational Behavior 11
(October 1977): 332-46.

Hughes, M. "Sex-Based Discrimination in Law Libraries." Law
Library Journal 64 (February 1971): 13-22.

Hunt, Janet G., and Hunt, Larry L. "Dilemmas and Contradictions of Status: The Case of the Dual-Career Family."
Social Problems 24 (April 1977): 407-16.

Huser, W. R., and Grant, C. W. "Study of Husbands and Wives
from Dual-Career and Traditional-Career Families." Psychology of Women Quarterly 3 (Fall 1978): 78-89.

Jarman, Betty Jane. "The Effect of Parental Messages on the
    Career Patterns of Professional Women." Ph.D. dissertation,
    California School of Professional Psychology, 1976.

Jerdee, Thomas H., and Rosen, Benson. Factors Influencing the
    Career Commitment of Women 1976. Bethesda, Md.: ERIC Docu-
    ment Reproduction Service, 1976. ED 132 665.

Johnson, Richard W. "Relationships between Female and Male
    Interest Scales for the Same Occupation." Journal of Voca-
    tional Behavior 11 (October 1977): 239-52.

Jusenius, Carol L. "The Influence of Work Experience and
    Typicality of Occupational Assignment on Women's Earnings."
    In U.S. Department of Labor, Dual Careers: A Longitudinal
    Analysis of the Labor Market Experience of Women volume 4,
    ed. by Herbert S. Parnes. Washington, D.C.: Govt. Print-
    ing Office, 1976.

Kanter, Rosabeth Moss. "The Impact of Hierarchical Structures
    on the Work Behavior of Women and Men." Social Problems
    23 (April 1976): 415-30.

__________. Men and Women of the Corporation. New York: Basic
    Books, 1977.

Kaplan, R., ed. American Minorities and Economic Opportunity.
    New York: Peacock Pr., 1977.

Kashket, Eva Ruth; Robbins, Mary Louise; Leive, Loretta; and
    Huang, Alice S. "Status of Women Microbiologists." Sci-
    ence 183 (February 8, 1974): 488-94.

Kaufman, Helen. "The Status of Women in Administration in
    Selected Institutions of Higher Education in the United
    States." Ph.D. dissertation, New York University, 1961.

Kievit, Mary Bach. A Review and Synthesis of Research in the
    World of Work. Washington, D.C.: Govt. Printing Office,
    1972.

Kim, Soon D., and Kim, Mary T. "Academic Library Research: A
    Twenty Year Perspective." In New Horizons for Academic Li-
    braries, pp. 375-83. New York: K. G. Saur, 1979.

King, Donald W.; Debons, Anthony; Mansfield, Una; and Shirey,
    Donald L. "A National Profile of Information Profession-
    als." Bulletin of the American Society of Information Sci-
    ence 6 (August 1980): 18-22.

King, Donald W.; Krauser, Cheri; and Sague, Virginia M.
    "Profile of ASIS Membership." Bulletin of the American So-
    ciety for Information Science 6 (August 1980): 9-17.

Knox, Margaret Euid. "Professional Development of Reference
    Librarians in a University Library: A Case Study." Ph.D.
    dissertation, University of Illinois, 1957.

Kohen, Andrew Ivor, et al. Women and the Economy: A Biblio-
    graphy and a Review of the Literature on Sex Differentiation
    in the Labor Market. Columbus: Center for Human Resource
    Research, Ohio State University, 1975.

Korb, G. M. "Successful Librarians as Revealed in Who's Who
    in America." Wilson Library Bulletin 20 (April 1946):
    603-4; 607.

Kronus, Carol T. "Women in Librarianship: The Majority Rules?"
    Protean 1 (1971): 4-9.
"LC Minority Employment, December, 1975." LC Information
    Bulletin 35 (January 23, 1976): 51.
Labb, J. "Librarians in Who's Who in America." Wilson
    Library Bulletin 25 (September 1950): 54-56.
Ladd, Jr., Everett Carll, and Lipset, Seymour Martin. The
    Divided Academy: Professors and Politics. New York:
    McGraw-Hill, 1975.
Lafky, Beth Louise. "Women's Intragenerational Occupational
    Mobility: A Retrospective Analysis of Career Patterns."
    Ph.D. dissertation, University of California, Riverside,
    1979.
Land, Kenneth C., and Spilerman, Seymour, eds. Social
    Indicator Models. New York: Russell Sage Foundation, 1975.
Landon, Glenda Lee. "Perceptions of Sex-Role Stereotyping and
    Women Teachers' Administrative Career Aspirations." Ph.D.
    dissertation, University of Wisconsin, 1975.
Larwood, Laurie; Wood, Marion M.; and Inderlied, Sheila
    Davis. "Training Women for Management: New Problems, New
    Solutions." Academy of Management Review 3 (July 1978):
    584-93.
Laumann, Edward O., ed. Social Stratification: Research and
    Theory for the 1970's. New York: Bobbs-Merrill, 1970.
Laurence, William, and Brown, Duane. "An Investigation of
    Intelligence, Self-Concept, Socio-economic Status, Race and
    Sex as Predictions of Career Maturity." Journal of Voca-
    tional Behavior 9 (August 1976): 43-52.
Lawler, E. E., III. Motivation in Work Organizations.
    Monterey, Calif.: Brooks/Cole, 1973.
Laws, Judith Long. "Work Aspiration of Women: False Leads and
    New Starts." Signs 1 (Spring 1976): 33-49.
Learmont, C. L. "Placements and Salaries 1979: Wider
    Horizons." Library Journal 105 (November 1980): 2271-77.
    ______, and Darling, R. "Placement and Salaries 1975: A
    Difficult Year." Library Journal 101 (July 1976): 1487-93.
    ______. "Placements and Salaries 1976: A Year of Adjustment."
    Library Journal 102 (June 15, 1977): 1345-51.
    ______. "Placements and Salaries 1977: The Picture
    Brightens." Library Journal 103 (July 1978): 1339-45.
    ______, and Troiano, Richard. "Placements and Salaries 1978:
    New Directions." Library Journal 104 (July 1979): 1415-22.
Leinbach, Anne E., and Beardwood, Louise B. "Greater
    Philadelphia Law Library Association 1979 Survey." Law Li-
    brary Journal 73 (Spring 1980): 498-505.
Leland, Carole Anne. "Women-Men-Work: Women's Career
    Aspirations as Affected by the Male Environment." Ph.D.
    dissertation, Stanford University, 1966.
Lenny, E. "Women's Self Confidence in Achievement Settings."
    Psychological Bulletin 84 (January 1977): 1-13.

Letarte, John Herbert. "Effect of Formal Study and Work
    Experience on the Occupational and Self Concepts of Librari-
    ans." Ed.D. dissertation, Columbia University, 1968.
Levine, Adeline. "Educational and Occupational Choice: A
    Synthesis of Literature from Sociology and Psychology."
    Journal of Consumer Research 2 (March 1976): 276-89.
    ______. "Forging a Feminine Identity: Women in Four Profes-
    sional Schools." American Journal of Psychoanalysis 35
    (Spring 1975): 63-67.
Levitt, Eleanor S. "A Study of Four Career Patterns and
    Associated Life History Characteristics among Female Pro-
    fessional Librarians." Ph.D. dissertation, New York Univer-
    sity, 1971.
Lewis, A. J. "1977 Statistical Survey of Law School Libraries
    and Librarians." Law Library Journal 71 (May 1978):
    318-55.
Lewis, Edwin C. Developing Women's Potential. Ames, Iowa:
    State University Pr., 1968.
Lipman-Blumen, Jean. "Toward a Homosocial Theory of Sex
    Roles: An Explanation of the Sex Segregation of Social In-
    stitutions." Signs 1 (Spring 1976): 15-31.
Lipow, Ann, et al. A Report on the Status of Women Employed
    in the Library of the University of California, Berkeley.
    Bethesda, Md.: ERIC Document Reproduction Service, 1971. ED
    066 163.
Lloyd, Cynthia B. "The Division of Labor Between the Sexes, a
    Review." In Sex, Discrimination, and the Division of Labor,
    pp. 1-26, ed. by Cynthia B. Lloyd. New York: Columbia Uni-
    versity Pr., 1975.
London, Manual; Cheney, Larry; and Tanis, Richard L. "The
    Relationship Between Cosmospolitan-Local Orientation and Job
    Performance." Journal of Vocational Behavior 11 (October
    1977): 182-95.
Long, Larry H. "Women's Labor Force Participation and the
    Residential Mobility of Families." Social Forces 52
    (March 1974): 342-48.
Long, M. L. The State Library Consultant at Work. Spring-
    field, Ill.: Illinois State Library, 1965.
Lowenthal, Helen. "1978 Update on Women in Libraries." Bay
    State Librarian 67 (Fall 1978): 21-23.
Luethe, Marie. The Status of Women and Ethnic Minorities
    Employed in the Libraries of the California State University
    and College System. Bethesda, Md.: ERIC Document Reproduc-
    tion Service, 1974. ED 127 984.
Lynn, Naomi; Vaden, Allene; and Vaden, Richard. "The
    Challenges of Men in a Women's World: Attitudes of Male and
    Female Administrators." Part II. Public Personnel Journal
    (January/February 1975): 12-17.
    ______. "Toward a Non-Sexist Personnel Opportunity Structure:
    The Federal Executive Bureaucracy." Public Personnel
    Management 8 (July/August 1979): 209-15.

McClendon, McKee J.   "The Occupational Status Attainment Processes of Males and Females." <u>American Sociological Review</u> 41 (February 1976): 52-64.

Maccoby, E. E., and Jacklin, C. N. <u>The Psychology of Sex Differences</u>. Stanford, Calif.: Stanford University Pr., 1974.

McGee, Jenny; Fazzone, Nancy; and Huston, Colleen. "Survey of New England Hospital Libraries." <u>Hospital Libraries</u> 5 (Spring 1980): 3-5.

McKenzie, Sheila Dereira. "A Comparative Study of Feminine Role Perception, Selected Personality Characteristics, and Traditional Attitudes of Professional Women and Housewives." Ph.D. dissertation, University of Houston, 1971.

McNally, Gertrude Bancroft. "Patterns of Female Labor Force Activity." <u>Industrial Relations</u> 7 (May 1968): 204-18.

Magrill, Rose Mary. "Occupational Image and the Choice of Librarianship as a Career." Ph.D. dissertation, University of Illinois at Champaign-Urbana, 1969.

Maloney, R. A. "The 'Average' Director of a Large Public Library." <u>Library Journal</u> 96 (February 1, 1971): 443-45.

Manchak, B. "ALA Salary Survey: Personal Members." <u>American Libraries</u> 2 (April 1971): 409-17.

Manhardt, P. J. "Job Orientation of Male and Female College Graduates in Business." <u>Personnel Psychology</u> 25 (Summer 1972): 361-68.

Marley, Sue. "A Comparative Analysis of Library Directorships in Four Midwestern States." <u>Focus on Indiana Libraries</u> 29 (Fall/Winter 1975): 4-6.

Marrett, Cora Bagley. "Centralization in Female Organizations: Reassessing the Evidence." <u>Social Problems</u> 19 (Winter 1972): 348-57.

Martin, Jean Krieg. "Factors Relating to the Representation of Women in Library Management." Master's thesis, University of Georgia, 1978.

Marwell, Gerald. "Why Ascription? Parts of a More or Less Formal Theory of the Functions and Dysfunctions of Sex Roles." <u>American Sociological Review</u> 40 (August 1975): 445-55.

________; Rosenfeld, Rachel; and Spilerman, Seymour. "Geographic Constraints on Women's Careers in Academia." <u>Science</u> 205 (September 1979): 1225-31.

________, et al. <u>Residence Location, Biographic Mobility and the Attainment of Women in Academia</u>. Institute for Research on Poverty Discussion Papers (August 1976): 359-76. Bethesda, Md.: ERIC Document Reproduction Service. ED 131 799.

Mason, Karen Oppenheim. "The Social Institutions of Occupational Segregation-Comment III." <u>Signs</u> 1 (Spring 1976): 81-83.

Mattfeld, Jacquelyn A., and Van Aken, Carol G. Women and the
    Scientific Professions. Cambridge, Mass.: MIT Pr., 1965.
Maynard, Cathleen E., and Zawacki, Robert A. "Mobility and
    the Dual Career Couple." Personnel Journal 58 (July
    1979): 468-72.
Merton, Robert K. Social Theory and Social Structure. New
    York: Free Press, 1968.
Middleton, Lorenzo. "Marriage Curbs Women's Careers in
    Academe, Sociologists Find." The Chronicle of Higher Educa-
    tion 19 (October 9, 1979): 1,17.
Miles, Leroy. "Implications for Women and Minorities."
    Vocational Guidance Quarterly 25 (June 1977): 356-63.
Miller, Sheila J. "Family Life Cycle, Extended Family
    Orientations, and Economic Aspirations as Factors in the
    Propensity to Migrate." The Sociological Quarterly 17
    (Summer 1976): 323-35.
Millman, Marcia, and Kanter, Rosabeth Moss. Another Voice.
    New York: Archer, 1977.
Molenda, Michael. "The Relationship of Sociodemographic
    Characteristics and Opinion to Political Participation in a
    Professional Association." Ph.D. dissertation, Syracuse
    University, 1971.
________, and Cambre, Marjorie. "The AECT Member Opinion
    Survey: Income Comparisons." Audiovisual Instruction 22
    (April 1977): 47-51.
________. "The 1976 Member Opinion Survey." Audiovisual
    Instruction 22 (March 1977): 65-69.
Morgan, Marilyn A. Managing Career Development. New York:
    Van Nostrand, 1980.
Morrison, P. D. "The Career of the Academic Librarian: A
    Study of the Social Origins, Educational Attainments, Voca-
    tional Experience, and Personality Characteristics of a
    Group of American Academic Librarians." Ph.D. dissertation,
    University of California, Berkeley, 1961.
________. "The Career of the Academic Librarian: A Study of
    the Social Origins, Educational Attainments, Vocational Ex-
    perience, and Personality Characteristics of a Group of
    American Academic Librarians." ACRL Monograph no. 29. Chi-
    cago: ALA, 1969.
________. "The Personality of the Academic Librarian." College
    and Research Libraries 24 (September 1963): 365-68.
Mortimer, Jeylan; Hall, Richard; and Hill, Reuben. "Husbands'
    Occupational Attributes as Constraints on Wives' Employ-
    ment." Sociology of Work and Occupations 5 (August 1978):
    285-313.
Muchinsky, Paul M., and Harris, Sharon L. "The Effect of
    Applicant Sex and Scholastic Standing on the Evaluation of
    Job Applicant Resumes in Sex-Typed Occupations." Journal of
    Vocational Behavior 11 (August 1977): 95-108.

Mulvey, Mary Crowly. "Psychological and Sociological Factors
    in Prediction of Career Patterns of Women." Genetic Psy-
    chology Monographs 68 (November 1963): 309-86.
"Music Library Association: Report of the Committee on Goals
    and Objectives, April 1975." MLA Notes 32 (September
    1975): 15-30.
Myers, Mildred S. "Mid-Career Special Librarian-Where Do We
    Go From Here?" Special Libraries 70 (July 1979): 263-71.
Nagely, D. L. "Traditional and Pioneer Working Mothers."
    Journal of Vocational Behavior 1 (October 1971): 331-41.
National Research Council. Office of Scientific Personnel.
    Research Division. Careers of Ph.Ds: Academic versus Non-
    academic, A Second Report on Follow-Up of Doctorate Cohorts
    1935-1960. Washington, D.C.: National Academy of Sciences,
    1968.

______. Profiles of Ph.D's in the Sciences: Summary Report
    on Follow-up of Doctorate Cohorts, 1935-1960. Washington,
    D.C.: National Academy of Sciences, 1965.
National Science Foundation. "Sex and Ethnic Differentials in
    Employment and Salaries among Federal Scientists and Engi-
    neers." Reviews of Data on Science Resources 34 (December
    1979): 1-11.
Niemi, Beth. "Geographic Immobility and Labor Force
    Mobility: A Study of Female Unemployment." ed. by Cynthia
    B. Lloyd. In Sex, Discrimination and the Division of Labor,
    pp. 6-89, ed. by Cynthia B. Lloyd. New York: Columbia Uni-
    versity Pr., 1975.
Nieva, Veronica F., and Gutek, Barbara A. "Sex Effects on
    Evaluation." Academy of Management Review 5 (April 1980):
    267-76.
1980 Association of American Library Schools: Library Educa-
    tion Statistical Report. State College, Pa.: Association of
    American Library Schools, October 1980.
"1980-81 Salaries by Rank and Discipline Group for Faculty
    Members on 9-Month or 10-Month Contracts." The Chronicle of
    Higher Education November 3, 1980, p.6.
Nilson, Linda Burzotta. "The Occupational and Sex Related
    Components of Social Standing." Ph.D. dissertation, Univer-
    sity of Wisconsin, Madison, 1974.
O'Connor, Daniel, and Van Orden, Phyllis. "Getting into
    Print." College and Research Libraries 39 (September
    1978): 389-96.
O'Leary, V. E. "Some Attitudinal Barriers to Occupational
    Aspirations in Women." Psychological Bulletin 81 (Novem-
    ber 1974): 809-26.
Olsgaard, John N., and Olsgaard, Jane Kinch. "Authorship in
    Five Library Periodicals." College and Research Libraries
    (January 1980): 49-53.
Oltman, Ruth M. Campus 1970: Where Do Women Stand? Washing-
    ton, D.C.: American Association of University Women, 1970.

O'Neil, James M.   "Holland's Theoretical Signs of Consistency and Differentiation and Their Relationship to Academic Potential and Achievement."   Journal of Vocational Behavior 11 (October 1977): 166-73.

______, and Magoon, Thomas M.   "The Predictive Power of Holland's Investigative Personality Type and Consistency Levels Using the Self Directed Search."   Journal of Vocational Behavior 10 (February 1977): 39-46.

Oppenheimer, Valerie.   "The Sex-Labeling of Jobs."   Industrial Relations 7 (1968): 219-34.

Orcutt, M. A., and Walsh, M. A.   "Traditionality and Congruence of Career Aspirations for College-Women."   Journal of Vocational Behavior 14 (February 1979): 1-11.

Osipow, Samuel H., ed.   Emerging Woman: Career Analysis and Outlooks.   Columbus, Ohio: Charles E. Merrill, 1975.

______.   Theories of Career Development.   New York: Appleton-Century-Crofts, 1973.

______.   "Vocational Behavior and Career Development, 1975: A Review."   Journal of Vocational Behavior 9 (October 1976): 129-45.

Osterman, Paul.   "Sex Discrimination in Professional Employment: A Case Study."   Industrial and Labor Relations Review 32 (July 1979): 451-64.

Panek, Paul E., and Rusl, Michael C.   "Current Sex Stereotypes of 25 Occupations."   Psychological Reports 40 (1977): 212-14.

Parnes, Herbert S., and Nestel, Gilbert.   "Factors in Career Orientation and Occupational Status."   In U. S. Department of Labor, Dual Careers: A Longitudinal Analysis of the Labor Market Experience of Women volume 4, pp. 57-95, ed. by Herbert S. Parnes.   Washington, D.C.: Govt. Printing Office, 1976.

Parrish, J. B.   "Women in Professional Training."   Monthly Labor Review 97 (May 1974): 41-43.

Parsons, Jerry L.   "Characteristics of Research Library Directors, 1958 and 1973, How Have They Changed?"   Wilson Library Bulletin 50 (April 1976): 613-17.

Patrick, Theodore A.   "Personality and Family Background Characteristics of Women Who Enter Male-Dominated Professions."   Ph.D. dissertation, Columbia University, 1973.

Patterson, Michelle.   "Alice in Wonderland: A Study of Women Faculty in Graduate Departments of Sociology."   American Sociologist 6 (August 1971): 226-36.

Paul, Carol Ann Bjork.   "Personal, Educational, and Career Patterns of Men and Women Administrators in the Massachusetts Community Colleges."   Ed.D. dissertation, Boston University, 1978.

Perrucci, Carolyn C., and Targ, Dena B.   "Early Work Orientation and Later Situational Factors as Elements of Work Commitment among Married-Women College Graduates."   Sociological Quarterly 19 (Spring 1978): 266-80.

Peterson, Gary T. "Instructional Media Graduates 1971-72."
    Audiovisual Instruction 18 (May 1973): 41-43.
    ______. "Graduates of Media Programs in 1972-73." _Audiovisual
    Instruction_ 19 (March 1974): 26-28.
    ______. "Graduates of Media Programs in 1973-74." _Audiovisual
    Instruction_ 20 (April 1975): 46-49.
    ______. "Job Picture Brighter for Graduates of Media Programs
    in 1974-75." _Audiovisual Instruction_ 21 (April 1976):
    9-11.
    ______. "Graduates of Media Programs 1975-76: An Optimistic
    Study." _Audiovisual Instruction_ 22 (April 1977): 19-21.
Peterson, Esther. "Working Women." _Daedalus_ 93 (Spring
    1964): 671-99.
Pettigrew, Nancy J., and Stepp, James M. "Employment Charac-
    teristics and Labor Force Participation of Female Graduates
    of Clemson University." _Bulletin of the South Carolina
    Agricultural Experiment Station_ 602 (October 1977).
Pietrofesa, John J., and Splette, Howard. _Career Develop-
    ment: Theory and Research_. New York: Grune & Stratton,
    1975.
Plate, Kenneth H., and Seigel, Jacob P. "Career Patterns of
    Ontario Librarians." _Canadian Library Journal_ 36 (June
    1979): 143-48.
Plost, M., and Rosen, M. J. "Effects of Sex of Career Models
    on Occupational Preferences of Adolescents." _AV Communica-
    tion Review_ 22 (Spring 1974): 41-50.
Pope, Beatrice Wooding. "Factors Influencing Career Aspira-
    tions and Development of Women Holding Administrative
    Positions in Public Schools." Ed.D. dissertation, Temple
    University, 1979.
Psathas, G. "Toward a Theory of Occupational Choice for
    Women." _Sociology and Social Research_ 52 (January 1968):
    252-70.
Quadagno, Jill Sobel. "Career Patterns of Men and Women
    Physicians: The Effect of Status-Set Typing." Ph.D. dis-
    sertation, University of Kansas, 1976.
Rapoport, Rhona, and Rapoport, Robert N. "The Dual Career
    Family." _Human Relations_ 22 (February 1969): 3-30.
    ______. "Early and Later Experiences as Determinates of Adult
    Behavior: Married Women's Family and Career Patterns."
    British Journal of Sociology 22 (March 1971): 16-30.
Rayman, Ronald, and Goudy, Frank William. "Research and Publi-
    cation Requirements in University Libraries." _College and
    Research Libraries_ (January 1980): 43-48.
Reagan, Agnes Lytton. _A Study of Factors Influencing College
    Students to Become Librarians_. ACRL Monograph 21. Chicago:
    ACRL, 1958.
Recely, Natalie, and Clark, L. "Level of Self-Esteem and
    Conformity to Sex-Role Stereotypes." Ph.D. dissertation,
    University of Colorado, 1973.

BIBLIOGRAPHY   72

"Recruiter Surveys: Computer Pros Are Hottest." Computer
    Careers News 2 (February 23, 1981): 7.
Reeling, Patricia A. "Undergraduate Student Characteristics
    as an Aid in Early Identification of Potential Librarians."
    New York: School of Library Service, Columbia University,
    1965. (Unpublished)
Regan, Carole Ann Bennett. "Attitudes towards Parents and
    Achievement Motivation of Freshmen Women in a Selective
    Urban University in Relation to Mother's Career Patterns."
    Ph.D. dissertation, University of Pennsylvania, 1972.
Reich, Carol. Occupational Segregation and Its Effects: A
    Study of Women in the Alberta Public Service. Ontario:
    Women Associates Consulting, Inc., 1979. (Mimeographed)
Rensel, Jeanne. "The Status of Women Librarians in Washington
    State." PNLA Quarterly 44 (Summer 1980): 18-25.
Renshawe, Michael L. "The Condition of the Law Librarian in
    1976." Law Library Journal 69 (November 1976): 627-29.
Rhodes, Leilia Gaston. "A Critical Analysis of the Career
    Backgrounds of Selected Black Female Librarians." Ph.D.
    dissertation, Florida State University, 1975.
Rideout, Anne H. "The Upward Mobility of Women in Higher
    Education: A Profile of Women Home Economics Administra-
    tors." Ph.D. dissertation, University of Massachusetts,
    1974.
Ritchie, Richard J., and Boehm, Virginia R. "Biographical
    Data as a Predictor of Women's and Men's Management Poten-
    tial." Journal of Vocational Behavior 11 (August 1977):
    363-68.
Ritchie, Shelia. Career Aspirations of Female Librarians in
    English Public Libraries. London: Elm Publications, 1978.
Roe, Anne. The Psychology of Occupations. New York: John
    Wiley, 1956.
Rose, Clare; Menninger, Sally Ann; and Nyre, Glenn F. The
    Study of the Academic Employment and Graduate Enrollment
    Patterns and Trends of Women in Science and Engineering:
    Summary. Los Angeles: Evaluation and Training Institute,
    1979.
Rose, H. A., and Elton, C. F. "Sex and Occupational Choice."
    Journal of Counseling Psychology 18 (September 1971):
    456-61.
Rosenberg, Morris. Occupations and Values. New York: Free
    Press, 1957.
Rosenfeld, Rachel A. "Women's Employment Patterns and Occupa-
    tional Achievements." Social Science Research 7 (March
    1978): 61-80.
________. "Women's Employment Patterns and Occupational Achieve-
    ments." Ph.D. dissertation, University of Wisconsin,
    Madison, 1976.
________. "Women's Intergenerational Occupational Mobility."
    American Sociological Review 43 (February 1978): 36-46.

Rossi, A. S. "Barriers to the Career Choice of Engineering,
Medicine, or Science among American Women." <u>Women and the
Scientific Professions</u>. Cambridge, Mass.: MIT Pr., 1965,
pp.51-127.

__________. "Status of Women in Graduate Departments of Sociol-
ogy, 1968-69." <u>American Sociologist</u> 5 (February 1970):
1-12.

__________. <u>Women Scientists: Problems and Prospects</u>. Chicago:
University of Chicago, Committee on Human Developments, 1966.

__________, and Calderwood, Ann, eds. <u>Academic Women on the Move</u>.
New York: Russell Sage Foundation, 1973.

Rubin, Dick. "Do American Women Marry Up?" <u>American Sociological Review</u> 33 (October 1968): 750-60.

Ryder, Norman. "The Cohort as a Concept in the Study of Social
Change." <u>American Sociological Review</u> 30 (December 1965):
843-61.

"SLA Salary Survey: 1970." <u>Special Libraries</u> 61 (July/Au-
gust 1970): 333-48.

"SLA Salary Survey: 1973." <u>Special Libraries</u> 64 (December
1973): 594-628.

"SLA Salary Survey: 1976." <u>Special Libraries</u> 67 (December
1976): 597-624.

"SLA Salary Survey: 1979." <u>Special Libraries</u> 70 (December
1979): 559-89.

"SLA 1980 Salary Survey Update." <u>Special Libraries</u> 71 (December 1980): 541.

Safilios-Rothchild, Constantina. "Dual Linkages between the
Occupational and Family Systems: A Macro-Sociological Analysis." <u>Signs</u> 1 (Spring 1976): 51-60.

__________. <u>Toward a Sociology of Women</u>. Lexington, Mass.: Xerox
College Publishing, 1972.

"Salary and Budget Survey." <u>Online</u> 3 (July 1979): 51-53.

Sawhill, Isabel. "Discrimination and Poverty among Women Who
Head Families." <u>Signs</u> 2 (Spring 1976): 201-11.

Scheresky, Ruth F. "Occupational Roles Are Sex-Typed by
Six-to Ten-Year Old Children." <u>Psychology in the Schools</u>
14 (April 1977): 220-24.

Schiller, Anita R. "Academic Librarians' Salaries." <u>College
and Research Libraries</u> 30 (March 1969): 101-11.

__________. <u>Characteristics of Professional Personnel in College
and University Libraries</u>. Research series no. 16. Spring-
field: Illinois State Library, 1969. (Also published as ED
020 766).

__________. "Women in Librarianship." <u>Advances in Librarianship</u>
4 (1974): 103-27.

Schlacter, Gail A. <u>Minorities and Women: A Guide to Reference Literature in the Social Sciences</u>. Los Angeles:
Reference Service Pr., 1977.

Sedney, Mary Anne, and Turner, Barbara F. "Test of Causal
Sequences in Two Models for Development of Career-Orien-

tation in Women." _Journal of Vocational Behavior_ 6 (June
1975): 281-91.

Seeliger, R. A. "Librarians in _Who's Who in America,
1956-1957._" Master's thesis, University of Texas, 1961.

Sell, Ralph R., and De Jong, Gordon F. "Toward a Motivational
Theory of Migration Decision Making." _Journal of Popula-
tion_ 1 (Winter 1978): 313-35.

Selvidge, Norma Jo. "Communication of Influence: Management
Style of Women Executives." Ph.D. dissertation, University
of Texas, 1977.

Sewell, William H.; Hallen, Archibald O.; and Ohlendorf,
George W. "The Educational and Early Occupation Status
Attainment Process." _American Sociological Review_ 35
(1970): 1014-27.

Shartle, Carroll L. _Occupational Information: Its Development and Application._ 3d ed. Englewood Cliffs, N.J.:
Prentice-Hall, 1959.

Shaw, Louise C. "1980 Salary Survey." _Datamation_ 26 (April
1980):110-18.

Shediac, Margaret. "Greater Philadelphia Law Library Association 1977 Survey." _Law Library Journal_ 71 (February
1978): 170-76.

______. "Private Law Libraries Special Interest Section 1979
Salary Survey." _Law Library Journal_ 73 (Winter 1980):
218-26.

Shelton, Barbara. "Feminism: Implications for Employment
Counselors." _Journal of Employment Counseling_ 13 (September 1976): 116-21.

Simon, Rita James; Clark, Shirley Merritt; and Galway,
Kathleen. "The Woman Ph.D.: A Recent Profile." _Social
Problems_ 15 (Fall 1967): 231-36.

Simpson, Richard L., and Simpson, Ida Harper. "Occupational
Choice among Career-Oriented College Women." _Marriage and
Family Living_ 23 (November 1961): 377-83.

______. "Women and Bureaucracy in the Semi-Professions." In
The Semi-Professions and Their Organization, ed. by Amitai
Etzioni. New York: Free Press, 1969.

Sink, Darryl L. "Beginning the Second Five Years." _Audio-
visual Instruction_ 23 (September 1978): 44-45.

______. "Employment Trends for Media Graduates: Business and
Industry Emerging." _Audiovisual Instruction_ 24 (September
1979): 36-37.

______. "Employment Trends for Media Graduates 1978-79." in
Educational Media Yearbook 1980, pp. 69-72, ed. by James W.
Brown and Shirley N. Brown. Littleton, Co.: Libraries Un-
limited, 1980.

Sixteen Reports on the Status of Women in the Professions.
New York: Professional Women's Caucus, 1970.

Slater, Margaret. "Career Patterns and Mobility in the
Library/Information Field." _ASLIB Proceedings_ 30 (Octo-
ber/November, 1978): 344-51.

______. Career Patterns and the Occupational Image: A Study
of the Library/Information Field. Occasional Paper no. 23.
London: ASLIB, 1979.

Slocum, Walter L. Occupational Careers. 2d ed. Chicago:
Aldine, 1974.

Sorensen, Aage B. "A Model for Occupational Careers." American Journal of Sociology 80 (July 1974): 44-57.

Stake, J. E. "Motives for Occupational Goal Setting among
Male and Female College Students." Journal of Applied Psychology 63 (October 1978): 617-22.

Stangl, P., and Hoke, W. N. A Survey of Salaries of Medical
School Librarians in the United States and Canada, 1976-77.
Stanford, Calif.: Stanford University, Lane Library, 1977.

Stein, A. H., and Bailey, M. M. "The Socialization of
Achievement Orientation in Females." Psychological Bulletin 80 (November 1973): 345-65.

Stevenson, Florence. "Women Administrators in Big Ten Universities." Ph.D. dissertation, Michigan State University,
1973.

Stone, Elizabeth W. Factors Related to the Professional
Development of Librarians. Metuchen, N.J.: Scarecrow Pr.,
1969.

Strober, Myra H. "Toward Dimorphics: A Summary Statement to
the Conference on Occupational Segregation." Signs 1
(Spring 1976): 293-302.

"Study of Academic Library Salaries in California." College
and Research Libraries News 10 (November 1978): 303.

Sukiennik, Adelaide Reno Weir. "Training Women Library School
Students for Greater Career Achievement." Ph.D. dissertation, University of Pittsburgh, 1978.

Sullivan, Peggy. "Women and Power." The Bookwoman 43 (1)
(April 1979): 5.

Super, Donald Edwin, ed. Career Development: Self-Concept
Theory. New York: College Entrance Examination Board, 1963.

______. The Psychology of Careers: An Introduction to Voca-
tional Development. New York: Harper, 1957.

______. "A Theory of Vocational Development." American
Psychologist 8 (1953): 185-90.

Sussman, Marvin B. and Betty E. Cogswell. "Family Influences
on Job Movement." Human Relations 24 (December 1971):
477-87.

Sweet, James A. Women in the Labour Force. New York: Seminar
Pr., 1973.

Talbot, Richard J., and von der Lippe, Ann. Salary Structures
of Librarians in Higher Education for the Academic Year
1975-1976. Chicago: ALA/ACRL, August 1976.

Tangri, Sandra Schwartz. "Determinants of Occupational Role
Innovation among College Women." Journal of Social Issues
28 (1972): 177-99.

______. "The Social Institutions of Occupational Segregation-Comment IV." _Signs_ 1 (Spring 1976): 84-86.

Taylor, Lee. _Occupational Sociology_. New York: Oxford University Pr., 1968.

Taylor, M. R. "External Mobility and Professional Involvement in Librarianship: A Study of the Careers of Librarians Graduating from Accredited Library Schools in 1955." Ph.D. dissertation, Rutgers University, 1973.

Terborg, James R. _Integration of Women into Management Positions: A Research Review_. Bethesda, Md.: ERIC Document Reproduction Service, 1976. ED 132 708.

______. "Women in Management: A Research Review." _Journal of Applied Psychology_ 62 (December 1977): 647-64.

Theodore, Athena, ed. _The Professional Woman_. Cambridge, Mass.: Schenkman Publishing, 1971.

Thomas, Emma Joahanne. "Career Patterns of Black Women Administrators in Historically Negro Senior Colleges and Universities." Ed.D. dissertation, Washington State University, 1976.

Tobias, Sheila. "Psychological and Social Barriers to Women on the Job." _Protean_ 1 (1971): 10-19.

Toman, W. _Family Constellation-Its Effects on Personality and Social Behavior_. 2d ed. New York: Springer, 1969.

Treiman, Donald J., and Terrell, Kermit. "Sex and the Process of Status Attainment: A Comparison of Working Women and Men." _American Sociological Review_ 40 (April 1975): 174-200.

"Two Steps Backward: Report on the Economic Status of the Profession, 1974-75." _AAUP Bulletin_ 61 (August 1975): 118-99.

Turner, Robert G., and Horn, Joseph M. "Personality, Husband-Wife Similarity and Holland's Occupational Types." _Journal of Vocational Behavior_ 10 (February 1977): 111-20.

U.S. Commission on Civil Rights. _Social Indicators of Equality for Minorities and Women_. Washington, D.C.: Govt. Printing Office, 1978.

U.S. Congress Joint Economic Committee. _American Women Workers in a Full Employment Economy_. Joint Committee Print. Washington, D.C.: Govt. Printing Office, 1977.

U.S. Department of Health, Education, and Welfare. _Library Statistics of Colleges and Universities: Institutional Data, Part B, Fall 1971: Basic Information on Collections, Staff, and Expenditures_. Washington, D.C.: Govt. Printing Office, 1972.

U.S. Department of Health, Education, and Welfare. _Library Statistics of Colleges and Universities Fall 1971: Analytic Report (Part C)_. Washington, D.C.: Govt. Printing Office, 1973.

U.S. Department of Labor, Bureau of Labor Statistics. _Library Manpower: A Study of Demand and Supply_. Bulletin 1852. Washington, D.C.: Govt. Printing Office, 1975.

U.S. Equal Employment Opportunity Commission. <u>Employment Profiles of Women and Minorities in 23 Metropolitan Areas: 1974</u>. Research Report no. 49, Washington, D.C.: Govt. Printing Office, 1976.

U.S. Equal Employment Opportunity Commission, Office of Research. <u>Employment Problems of Women: A Classic Example of Discrimination</u>, by Melvin Humphrey and Melba L. Lee. Research Report no. 37. Washington, D.C.: Govt. Printing Office, 1972.

U.S. Office of Education, National Center for Education Statistics. <u>Digest of Education Statistics: 1980</u>. Washington, D.C.: Govt. Printing Office, 1980.

U.S. Office of Personnel Management, Office of Intergovernmental Personnel Program. <u>State Salary Summary</u>. Washington, D.C.: Govt. Printing Office, 1973.

University of Pittsburgh. <u>Manpower Requirements in Scientific and Technical Communication: An Occupational Survey of Information Professionals</u>. (Prepared in conjunction with King Research, Inc. for National Science Foundation Project DSI-7727115). Pittsburgh: University of Pittsburgh, School of Library and Information Science, 1980.

Valentine, D.; Ellinger, N.; and Williams, M. "Sex-Role Attitudes and the Career Choices of Male and Female Graduate Students." <u>Vocational Guidance Quarterly</u> 24 (1975): 48-53.

Van Alstyne, Carol, et al. <u>Women and Minorities in Administrations of Higher Education Institutions: Employment Patterns and Salary Comparisons</u>. Washington, D.C.: College and University Personnel Association, June 1977.

Vetter, Betty M. "Working Women Scientists and Engineers." <u>Science</u> 207 (January 4, 1980): 28-34.

Vetter, Louise, and Stockburger, David W. <u>Career Patterns of a National Sample of Women</u>. Research and Development Series no. 95 (Reissue) Final Report. Columbus: Ohio State University, Columbus Center for Vocational Education, 1977.

Vice, Jackie Ann. "Career Development of Women in Engineering: Factors Influencing a Nontraditional Career." Ph.D. dissertation, Ohio State University, 1977.

Wahba, Susanne P. "Librarian Job Satisfaction, Motivation and Performance: An Empirical Test of Two Alternative Theories." Ph.D. dissertation, Columbia University, 1978.

________. "A Longitudinal Study of Career Pay of Men and Women Librarians." <u>LACUNY Journal</u> 4 (Fall 1975): 13-18.

Wallace, Phyllis Ann. <u>Equal Employment Opportunity and the A.T. and T. Case</u>. Cambridge, Mass.: MIT Pr., 1976.

Walsh, Patricia Ann. "Career Patterns of Women Administrators in Higher Education Institutions in California." Ph.D. dissertation, University of California, Los Angeles, 1975.

Walsh, W. Bruce, et al. "Holland's Theory and College Degreed Working Men and Women." <u>Journal of Vocational Behavior</u> 10 (April 1977): 180-85.

______. "Vocational Behavior and Career Development, 1978: A
Review." Journal of Vocational Behavior 15 (October
1979): 119-54.

Wanous, John P. "Organizational Entry: Newcomers Moving from
Outside to Inside." Psychological Bulletin 84 (July
1977): 601-18.

Ward, Patricia Layzell. Women and Librarianship: An Investigation into Certain Problems of Library Staffing. London:
Library Association, 1966.

Watson, Paula DeSimone. "Publication Activity among Academic
Librarians. "College and Research Libraries 38 (September
1977): 375-84.

Weaver, Charles N. "Sex Differences in the Determinants of
Job Satisfaction. "Academy of Management Journal 21 (June
1978): 265-74.

Weibel, Kathleen, and Heim, Kathleen M. The Role of Women in
Librarianship 1876-1976: The Entry, Advancement, and Strug-
gle for Equalization in One Profession. With assistance
from Dianne J. Ellsworth. Phoenix: Oryx Pr., 1979. (A
Neal-Schuman Professional Book)

Weil, Mildred W. "An Analysis of the Factors Influencing
Married Women's Actual or Planned Work Participation."
American Sociological Review 26 (1961): 91-96.

Weiss, Jane A.; Ramirez, Francisco O.; and Tracy, Terry.
"Female Participation in the Occupational System: A Comparative Institutional Analysis." Social Problems 23 (June
1976): 593-608.

Wiener, Yoash, and Gechman, Arthur S. "Commitment: A
Behavioral Approach to Job Involvement." Journal of Vocational Behavior 10 (February 1977): 47-52.

Wilkins, Barratt. Survey of State Library Agencies, 1977.
University of Illinois Occasional Paper no. 142. Urbana,
Ill.: Graduate School of Library Science, December 1979.

Williams, D., and King, M. "Sex Role Attitudes and Fear of
Success as Correlates of Sex Role Behavior." Journal of
College Student Personnel 17 (March 1976): 480-84.

Williams, G. "Trends in Occupational Differentiation by
Sex." Sociology of Work and Occupations 3 (February
1976): 38-62.

Williams, Martha; Ho, Liz; and Fielder, Lucy. "Career
Patterns: More Grist for Women's Liberation." Social Work
19 (July 1974): 463-66.

Williams, Patricia Jean. "Career Aspirations of Selected
Women Teachers as Related to Their Perceptions of the
Chances of Success in Becoming a School Administrator."
Ed.D. dissertation, University of North Colorado, 1977.

Winkler, Mary C. "The Life Styles of Women with Earned
Indiana University Doctorates." Ph.D. dissertation, Indiana
University, 1968.

Wolf, Wendy Carolyn. "Occupational Attainment of Married
     Women: Do Career Contingencies Matter?" Ph.D. disserta-
     tion, Johns Hopkins University, 1975.
Wolfson, Stanley M. "Salaries of Municipal Officials for
     1979." The Municipal Yearbook 1980. Washington, D.C.:
     International City Management Association, 1980: 83-108.
"Women's Program Statistical Update 1978: Grade Gap Narrows
     Slightly, More Women in Managment." Library of Congress
     Information Bulletin 38 (June 8, 1979): 210-12.
"Women's Program Statistical Update: 1979." LC Information
     Bulletin 39 (July 4, 1980): 238-40.
"Women's Program Statistical Update: 1980." LC Information
     Bulletin 40 (April 3, 1981): 109-12.
Wyant, June F. "Librarians and Career Planning." Special
     Libraries 65 (April 1974): 176-79.
Yohalem, Alice M. The Careers of Professional Women:
     Commitment and Conflict Final Report. New York: Columbia
     University, March 1978.
     ______. The Careers of Professional Women: Commitment and
     Conflict. Montclair, N.J.: Allanheld Osmon, 1979.
Yu, Miriam. "An Exploratory Study of Women in Traditionally
     Male Professions and Traditionally Female Professions, and
     the Role of Creativity in Their Career Choices." Ph.D. dis-
     sertation, University of Michigan, 1972.
Zytowski, Donald G. "Vocational Behavior and Career Develop-
     ment." Journal of Vocational Behavior 13 (October 1978):
     141-62.

Index

EVERYBODY

FOR

PRESIDENT

Everything you need to know
to run for the highest office
in the land

*Gil Campbell and Martha Gorman
with Michael Cader
(a well-placed source)*

Illustrated by Phil Scheuer

Workman Publishing, New York

Library of Congress Cataloging in Publication Data:

Campbell, Gil.
Everybody for president.

1. Political satire, American. 2. Presidents—United
States—Election—Anecdotes, facetiae, satire, etc.
I. Gorman, Martha. II. Title.
PN6231.P6C36 1984   818'.5407   84-7269
ISBN 0-89480-761-7 (pbk.)

Workman Publishing Company
1 West 39 Street
New York, NY 10018

Manufactured in the United States of America
First published by Idea Shop Printing Co. February 1984

First published by Workman Publishing April 1984

10   9   8   7   6   5   4   3   2   1